The Fashion Coloring Book

Attention: Every effort has been made to reproduce the colors on the facing page as accurately as possible. Due to the limitations of the four-color printing process, however, certain discrepancies are unavoidable. The color samples should therefore be used only as a guideline.

The Fashion Coloring Book

Sharon Lee Tate

Mona Shafer Edwards

1817

HARPER & ROW, PUBLISHERS, New York
Cambridge, Philadelphia, San Francisco,
London, Mexico City, São Paulo, Singapore, Sydney

Sponsoring Editor: Fred Henry
Project Editor: Nora Helfgott
Text Design: Robert Sugar
Cover Design: Mona Shafer Edwards
Production Manager: Jeanie Berke
Compositor: ComCom Division of Haddon Craftsmen, Inc.
Printer and Binder: The Murray Printing Company

The Fashion Coloring Book

Library of Congress Cataloging in Publication Data

Tate, Sharon Lee.
  The fashion coloring book.

  1. Fashion drawing. 2. Costume design. I. Edwards,
Mona Shafer, 1951– . II. Title.
TT509.T38 1985   741.67′2   84-4512
ISBN 0-06-046612-X

84 85 86 87 9 8 7 6 5 4 3 2

To Fred Henry,
whose ideas and constant encouragement
inspired this book

CONTENTS

How to Use This Book   *ix*
Preface   *xi*

1 CLOTHING: THE SILENT LANGUAGE   *2*
2 LEARNING TO SEND THE RIGHT MESSAGE   *4*
3 FASHION'S ROLE IN DRESSING   *6*
4 SUCCESSFUL CLOTHING FOR THE BUSINESS WOMAN   *8*
5 THE CLOSET CASE   *10*
6 THE BARE ESSENTIALS   *12*
7 THE BALANCED FIGURE   *14*
8 THE PEAR-SHAPED FIGURE   *16*
9 THE TOP-HEAVY FIGURE   *18*
10 COLOR   *20*
11 PERSONAL COLOR   *22*
12 MAKEUP COLOR   *24*
13 COLORING YOUR WARDROBE   *26*
14 CLOTHING SELECTION   *29*
15 FASHION COLORS   *38*

COLOR PROFILES   *41*

16 RED   *42*
17 PINK   *44*
18 ORANGE   *46*
19 BROWN   *48*
20 GREEN   *50*
21 BLUE   *52*
22 PURPLE   *54*
23 YELLOW   *56*
24 BLACK   *58*
25 GREY   *60*
26 WHITE   *62*

27 COLOR ILLUSIONS   *64*
28 PROPORTION   *76*
29 PROPORTION ILLUSIONS   *78*
30 PANT PROPORTION   *80*
31 HORIZONTAL PROPORTIONS   *82*
32 LINE   *84*
33 VERTICAL STYLE LINES   *86*
34 HORIZONTAL STYLE LINES   *88*
35 THE MOST IMPORTANT HORIZONTAL —THE HEMLINE   *90*

36 DIAGONAL STYLE LINES   *92*
37 CURVED LINES   *94*
38 FACE, NECK, AND SHOULDER SHAPES   *96*
39 SYMMETRY   *98*
40 SCALE   *100*
41 UNITY   *102*
42 FABRIC UNITY   *104*
43 RHYTHM   *106*
44 EMPHASIS: COLOR CONTRAST   *108*
45 EMPHASIS: DESIGN MOTIFS   *110*
46 SILHOUETTE   *112*
47 NATURAL SILHOUETTE: CLASSIC BATHING SUITS   *114*
48 NATURAL SILHOUETTE: NOVELTY BATHING SUITS   *116*
49 SLIM-LINE SILHOUETTE: PANTS   *118*
50 SLIM-LINE SILHOUETTE: SKIRTED OUTFITS   *120*
51 SOFT SILHOUETTE: PANTS   *122*
52 SOFT SILHOUETTE: SKIRTED OUTFITS   *124*
53 WEDGE SILHOUETTE   *126*
54 HOURGLASS SILHOUETTE   *128*
55 FULL-VOLUME SILHOUETTE: SKIRTED OUTFITS   *130*
56 FULL-VOLUME SILHOUETTE: PANTS   *132*
57 FABRIC   *134*
58 FIBERS   *136*
59 WEIGHT AND HAND   *138*
60 PATTERN: SCALE   *140*
61 PATTERN MOTIFS   *142*
62 PATTERNED FABRICS   *144*
63 PATTERN COMBINATIONS   *146*
64 FOUNDATIONS: THE BRA   *148*
65 OTHER FOUNDATIONS   *150*
66 PROPER FIT   *152*
67 FIT FOR THE LARGER FIGURE   *154*
68 FIT: TOPS AND SLEEVES   *156*
69 CONSTRUCTION: TAILORED JACKETS   *158*
70 CONSTRUCTION: DETAILS   *160*
71 CONSTRUCTION: SOFT GARMENTS   *162*

72   ACCESSORIES: SHOES   *164*
73   ACCESSORIES: STOCKINGS   *166*
74   ACCESSORIES: HANDBAGS   *168*
75   ACCESSORIES: JEWELRY   *170*
76   ACCESSORIES: BELTS   *172*
77   ACCESSORIES: HATS   *174*
78   ACCESSORIES: SCARVES   *176*

FIGURE CHARTS

1   BALANCED FIGURE: THIN   *178*
2   BALANCED FIGURE: AVERAGE   *179*
3   BALANCED FIGURE: LARGE   *180*
4   PEAR-SHAPED FIGURE: THIN   *181*
5   PEAR-SHAPED FIGURE: AVERAGE   *182*
6   PEAR-SHAPED FIGURE: LARGE   *183*
7   FULL-BUSTED FIGURE: THIN   *184*
8   FULL-BUSTED FIGURE: AVERAGE   *185*
9   FULL-BUSTED FIGURE: LARGE   *186*
10   TALL FIGURE   *187*
11   PETITE FIGURE   *188*
12   LONG WAISTED AND SHORT WAISTED   *189*
13   BROAD SHOULDERS AND NARROW SHOULDERS   *190*
14   LONG NECK AND SHORT, THICK NECK   *191*
15   PREGNANT FIGURE   *192*

HOW TO USE THIS BOOK

You will need some art supplies to work with this book.

1. *Medium-wide felt-tip pens.* Select a package of at least 16 colors. The more colors you have, the more variety your pictures can have.
2. *Colored pencils.* Purchase the kind with a soft base, such as Prismacolor. Buy several flesh tones and 12 to 34 additional colors, as your budget allows. You can color with the pencils and the felt-tip pens, using the pencils for small details and shading.
3. *Pad of tracing paper, 8 × 12 minimum size.* The paper will make it easy for you to copy illustrations so you can try other color combinations. Vellum or lightweight bond paper will also do the trick.
4. *Fine-line black marking pencil and #2 lead pencil.* These will be used to copy figures from the book for additional style line or color experiments.

One of the first subjects in the book is finding your personal color palette, that is, makeup and clothing colors that flatter your complexion. Alter the coloring suggestions so you color each page in your own palette. For example, an illustration that calls for a burgundy shade would be appropriate for a moon glow or blue-tone complexion. A person with a sunlight or yellow-tone complexion would use deep rust instead in the same illustration. Alternative colors for the two palettes are listed here to help you convert the color instructions to fit your palette.

Moon Glow (Blue-Tone Complexion)	Sunlight (Yellow-Tone Complexion)
Blue-red	Red-orange
Burgundy	Deep rust
Magenta	Cranberry
Pink	Watermelon
None	Orange
Light burgundy	Terra cotta
Pink	Peach
Taupe	Camel
Dark brown	Chocolate
Khaki	Warm beige
Grass green	Forest green
Blue-green, teal	Olive drab (OD)
Sky blue	Periwinkle
Royal blue	Cobalt blue
Aqua	Turquoise
Blue-violet	Red-violet
Pale yellow	Sunlight yellow, marigold
Blue-grey	Charcoal
Pearl grey	Cream, pale ivory
White	Cream
Dark navy	Bright navy

FIGURE CHARTS

The figure charts at the back of the book provide solutions at a glance to various figure problems. The first charts summarize flattering clothing solutions for the balanced, pear-shaped, and full-busted figures of several different weights. These guidelines will help people with these body types emphasize the positive and disguise the negative aspects of their appearance. Next, suggestions that maximize figure assets of petite and tall women are given. And finally, apparel ideas for women who want to camouflage specific body characteristics, such as long waists and narrow shoulders, are presented.

PREFACE

This book was written for four reasons: (1) to teach you the secrets of professional designers, (2) to help you develop a visual identity, (3) to show you how to save money by preplanning wardrobe purchases to avoid the expensive "mistakes" that sabotage a master clothing plan, and (4) to demonstrate that the skills and creativity involved in producing and controlling your visual image can be fun. Fashion at its best should always have an element of excitement and anticipation. It is worth investing time and practice in apparel selection to look your best because clothing that maximizes your physical assets helps you succeed both personally and professionally.

This is a *coloring* book for a special reason. When you read something, you receive a mental message. Combining the physical activity of coloring with this mental process reinforces the lesson being discussed. Use this book when you have a quiet moment, and let your mind imagine various solutions to the clothing problems presented. Think of yourself or the person whose wardrobe you are planning when you color a figure. Trace the figures several times and try different color schemes, then picture yourself in the garment. Professional fashion designers create styles by envisioning what an article of clothing will look like before it is made. They combine art principles with many trial-and-error garments and can envision the potential creation by just looking at and feeling a piece of fabric. With practice you too can develop this sixth sense and use it to select the most flattering apparel possible.

Begin planning your wardrobe by evaluating your life-style and body image. It is important to study your body objectively and to appreciate your good points. Improve aspects of your figure that require improvement, and discard prejudices about your body that do not pertain to visible faults. You are a valuable person, and developing an appropriate style of dressing will maximize your assets and allow you to be at your best. Truly chic people can forget what they are wearing because they have style and their clothing does not compete with their unique personalities.

The most expensive clothes you will ever buy are those that you do not wear often or that make you feel uncomfortable. You can dress successfully and economically by purchasing garments that are functional, stylish, comfortable, and flattering. Defining your clothing needs by matching them to your varied life-style and environment will free you to shop with a master plan. You will not be tempted by a persuasive salesperson or lured into purchasing an inappropriate garment because it is marked down. You will confidently choose clothing that fits into your wardrobe plan and is a true fashion investment.

You are not alone in trying to maximize your appearance. Seek advice from makeup and hair stylists. Shop in the best stores even if you are "just looking" and have to purchase more moderate items elsewhere. Develop your personal "taste level," and try developing a new image. Women's magazines often do make-over articles that are fascinating because an average-looking woman often blossoms into a beauty. This could be you. Try it!

Using *The Fashion Coloring Book* should be an experience of self-discovery and creativity. The tricks of the trade discussed in this book will help you make your wardrobe work for you. Remember, fashion is fun. A sense of humor and the self-assurance that comes from knowing your figure and your personal styling formula will free *you* to look and feel your best.

Sharon Lee Tate
Mona Shafer Edwards

The Fashion Coloring Book

1 CLOTHING: THE SILENT LANGUAGE

Appearance says a great deal about a person before a word is spoken. The image you project may be one of competence, confidence, and tranquillity. But, appearance may also signal the fact that a person's goal in life is low, that she lacks self-esteem, and that she need not be taken seriously. Looks reflect personality, moods, and feelings. Clothing and grooming elicit an instant reaction, and often there is no second chance to correct a misconception because our modern world demands speedy conclusions. Does putting this much emphasis on appearance strike you as shallow? How can others judge a person's inner self with a casual glance?

The importance of clothing in social relations has ancient roots. The decorative aspect of apparel was as important in early societies as its functional aspect. Clothes set apart the most prominent men in the tribe. The chief was designated by an elaborate headdress, fine robes, and other rich ornaments. The warrior applied paint to frighten his opponents and to declare his readiness for battle. The priest's vocation and rank were attested to by garments of ritual significance. Through the ages clothing and ornament have been used to distinguish one person from another and declare at a glance the status and often the wealth and occupation of a person.

Appearance, then, reflects who a person is and what he or she wants. Benjamin Franklin advised, "Eat what you like, but dress for other people." Successful people learn the language of clothing. They learn how to manipulate their appearance to conform to the expectations of their peer group and to generate favorable reactions. They know that first impressions can often have a lasting effect. "Look the part" is an expression that focuses on the importance of dressing to your goals and understanding the message your appearance is sending to others.

Do not confuse a desirable appearance with beauty. A person does not have to be beautiful to appear confident, powerful, or successful. Appearance is the total impression created by physical characteristics, emotional state, and apparel. When you look at someone, 80 to 90 percent of what you see is the person's apparel. It is the most important signal that attracts or warns people away in an initial contact.

Self-evaluation is the first step toward a desirable appearance. Each woman should discover and emphasize the positive aspects of her physical appearance. At the same time, she must recognize her shortcomings and learn how to minimize them. She must also learn to understand the nonverbal language of clothing. People who do not consider the message their clothing carries may un-

consciously dress to reflect how they secretly feel about themselves. They ignore the positive and negative aspects of their appearance and dress to reflect their moods. This unplanned visual presentation often carries a message of failure, unhappiness, and dissatisfaction with self and life. This message is a turn-off to other people.

Consciously dressing to elicit the positive reaction of others is not a dishonest action. It is a way to encourage people to regard you with interest. It is an invitation to explore the interesting and dynamic person that is behind a well-presented visual image.

Cream
& Navy
Stripe

Dusty
Rose

Red-
Brown

Burgundy

Bright
Red

Glance quickly at the three
women on this page. What is
the first impression you had
about each one's occupation,
personality (confident,
aggressive, bored, exciting,
competent, dull), and goals?

As you color the outfits,
notice your initial reactions to
the hue of red you are using.
Does the intensity and shade of
a color alter its impact and
change its image?

Brown

Burgundy

2 LEARNING TO SEND THE RIGHT MESSAGE

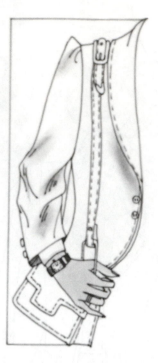

You are invited to a dinner party at the home of your boss. It is important that you make a good impression because you hope to be promoted out of a secretarial position. The invitation says casual, and you select a tailored suit and understated accessories that you hope will signal, "I am a serious person; I am efficient and competent." When you arrive at the house, the opening door reveals an informally clad hostess in a fashionable outfit. You feel dowdy and uncomfortable in your serious outfit. As you enter the room, people glance up and determine that you are indeed "serious," but at the wrong time. This was an opportunity for you to have dressed informally with a flare that would state, "I am your equal. I understand executive life-styles." You have misread the situation and clearly labeled yourself as a person who is not familiar with the social environment of the upwardly mobile position that you aspire to. A person tends to withdraw or to overact to conceal the feeling of being inappropriately dressed for a particular situation. Your behavior is influenced, and you are not able to act naturally. This situation could have been avoided by researching the event. You could have checked with the hostess about the degree of formality of the event or asked co-workers about what to expect. Realize that business clothing, worn off the job, diminishes the impact of its authority.

Avoid sending conflicting messages with your appearance. Signaling something that is incompatible with your role in a specific situation will confuse and distract your audience. Clothing is your personal advertisement to the world about your individuality and your goals. A successful personal advertising campaign begins with learning what effect your appearance has on others and becoming sensitive to your peers so your appearance is appropriate for specific situations.

People expect the situation and the personality of a person to be consistent with the projected image. Consider the following cases that describe successful and unsuccessful visual statements.

1. A woman wears a tight skirt and a revealing blouse to her job as a secretary. She is constantly fielding passes from the men and complains of harrassment. No matter how efficient and competent this woman is, others will read the message, "Think of me in sexual terms. The work that I do is secondary." Image and goals are incompatible. The image sends one message, but the person's goals are quite different.
2. A middle management woman wears conservative suits, sensible shoes, demure polyester blouses, and low-key accessories. She wonders why male and female contemporaries are promoted over her, even though she does a competent and efficient job. This woman is sending the message, "I am content to spend my time here as a worker, and this job suits my abilities." Her situation reflects the image she projects; nothing outstanding distinguishes this person from her competition. If her goal is advancement, she has made an unsuccessful statement.
3. An upwardly mobile woman has her eye on a promotion. She carefully analyzes how the people in the position she aspires to dress and recognizes their "symbols of power." Typically, these symbols include expensive, fashionably tailored garments and expensive briefcases and personal accessories. She invests in clothing and accessories that give her an executive look. She maintains her good performance and at the same time begins to look like she is headed for more important duties. Her new image adds to her self-confidence, and soon she has secured the promotion. This woman used her appearance to make a clear statement of her goal of advancement. Her image enhanced her personality and improved the reality of her situation.

A person must learn to be aware of the clothing message she is sending and to relate it to her audience. The clothing message must evolve as the person does. Changes must be made for different locations and different situations. Subtle nuances are especially important in more sophisticated situations. A woman who is competing in a male-dominated business must dress for men. Her presentation will be different if she works in a woman-dominated industry and is evaluated by feminine success standards. Plan your personal advertising campaign by learning to send the right messages through your appearance.

Pink

Pale Yellow

Brown

Red

Black, White, and Red Print

Brown Plaid

Pink and Grey Stripe

Black

Brown

Pink

Black

All of these women are wearing the skirted suit. Cut, fit, color, and style determine if the look is sexy, efficient but dull, or confident and fashionable. Which woman looks most likely to be promoted up the corporate ladder?

3 FASHION'S ROLE IN DRESSING

Fashion can be defined as what a specific group of people wear during a given time period. This simple definition does not hint at the bewilderment many people feel when trying to apply commercial fashion information to their personal life-style and appearance goals. Fashion is change, and change is confusing to many people. The commercial fashion industry is a vast and complicated system for creating and selling apparel. Retailers and manufacturers vary their messages in an attempt to appeal to potential customers who differ in life-style, age, occupation, size, and disposable income. A person who tries to interpret all the available fashion messages for her own self-image faces an awesome and futile task. Much confusion is eliminated when a person can analyze her physical type, can identify the needs of her situation, and can define the nonverbal message she wishes to send. Focus eliminates many alternatives that are inappropriate choices for a particular image.

Understanding the fashion cycle is an important first step in making your selections from merchandise offerings. A new silhouette or trend usually starts in higher-priced, more experimental garments that are often produced in Europe. These clothes are usually radical departures from the then current style, so they create excitement. This shock value makes news, and the outfits are featured in advertisements and editorials in fashion magazines and newspapers. Readers may lament, "Who would wear that!" There are always some "fashion victims

(FV)," a tongue-in-cheek label invented by *Women's Wear Daily,* the leading American fashion newspaper, to describe women who slavishly wear fashions for the sake of novelty. However, the very forward fashions are rarely translated directly into street wear. The most successful of the new ideas are interpreted into more commercial garments. High-priced designers, usually in the domestic markets, refine the new concepts and interpret them for more wearable clothing. This category of merchandise still uses high-quality fabric and styling details, but is more appropriate for American women.

The most successful trends in the high-price, designer market are then adapted for the middle-level market. By this time retailers have been able to test the new ideas on the American public. Styles that have not sold are discarded, and the best sellers are copied (called "knock-offs" in the trade) or reinterpreted. This merchandise sells to a customer who wants to look updated but not radical and does not want to pay designer prices for her clothing. The most successful of the new style may become classics. Classics are garments that are reinterpreted year after year because they are flattering and appropriate for many figures and occasions.

The mass merchandisers step in at this point and knock off the most successful styles from the moderate market in inexpensive fabrics. The high fashion elements of the style are usually still further modified so the garments will appeal to a vast number of people who can purchase them at a low price.

Finally, the style hits the mark-down racks and the least expensive retailers. The fabrications are very low quality, the style goes into decline, and it is closed out.

It is important to remember that manufacturers, designers, and retailers are in business to make money. They have to create and select merchandise that sells. They are not trying to lead the customer astray, only to stimulate her to continue to buy clothing. Merchandise is created for many different kinds of people. Creating a successful fashion image depends on focusing on the apparel that will provide the elements of dress that are most correct for your goals and life-style.

The high fashion garment stimulates designers of more commercial lines to select the most distinctive details and modify them for the American consumer. The influence of a fuller sleeve could be applied to blouses as well as a jacket.

White

Navy

Olive Green

Brightly Colored Print

4 SUCCESSFUL CLOTHING FOR THE BUSINESS WOMAN

More women are entering the job market than ever before. These women are often working to feed and clothe themselves and their children or to supplement their husband's income. They are saving to achieve the traditional American dream of home ownership. The traditional low-income, care-oriented service careers like teaching and nursing continue to attract the majority of working women, but an increasing number are turning toward careers that compete with men. Business demands a different attitude and appearance from the woman who seeks to move up the corporate ladder and into a profession. Her visual agenda must be different from her sisters'.

John T. Molloy has carefully studied the effectiveness of various kinds of apparel for business women and reports on the test results in *The Woman's Dress for Success Book.* He advocates a business uniform for women of the skirted suit in a conservative color. Molloy contends that this basic apparel gives business women a look of authority. He separates the business wardrobe from clothing for other occasions. Molloy's tests indicate that women should not dress like men, but they should use the idea of the male business suit to guide them in assembling a work wardrobe. The uniform will free them from the dictates of fashion and allow them to focus on an authoritative image conducive to establishing feminine authenticity within the business world.

Conservative businesses often dictate what their executives should wear by issuing a dress code. In some cases items in a wardrobe are specified, and various kinds of apparel become badges of rank. More often the guidelines are subtler and less easy to define. Geographical location and the type of industry will modify the criteria for a specific business uniform. In *Games Mother Never Taught You,* Betty Harragan suggests that an upwardly mobile business woman should study women and men at the level she aspires to and emulate their appearance.

It would be out of place, for example, to dress in a conservative navy suit, white blouse, and basic pumps if the male executives in your office wear fashion jeans, expensive suede jackets, and leather boots. The woman executive in this situation should adopt a more casual uniform, taking her cue from the accepted garb of the men in authority. Women who work in the fashion industry have a different visual orientation. Their superiors, who incidentally are often women rather than men, understand and value experimental fashion.

The key to understanding which visual symbols aid your upward mobility in a business setting is to observe the people at the levels around you. Consciously separate yourself from the lower-echelon women on the job. Dress like a secretary, and your chances of remaining one increase tremendously. It will be difficult to overcome the image your clothing projects. Your clothing should proclaim that you are a self-confident, able, ambitious person who is a team player within the framework of the established business organization.

Adopting the skirted suit as a business uniform does not mean that a person can ignore fashion messages and simply put on a conservative skirt, blazer, and blouse. Men's suits involve a complicated mixture of quality, classic styling, and current look that is important to recognize. Fashion cycles have stimulated many women to value variety over quality. They may spend a large amount of money for many items. The business woman who wants to succeed must change her attitude and emphasize quality over quantity. She should invest more money per item and purchase fewer clothes when funds are limited. Male executives value quality and understand fabric, fit, and detailing. They will transfer these judgments to their female co-worker's clothing. Quality fabric and detailing are usually found in more expensive clothing and cannot be easily faked. Accessories can vary the uniform and make it distinctive and yet appropriate for the business climate. Career apparel can rarely be selected from the most innovative fashions but should be selected for a current look.

SALLY FORTH　　　　　　　　**by Greg Howard**

Sally Forth by Greg Howard. Copyright © 1982 Field Enterprises, Inc. Courtesy of Field Newspaper Syndicate.

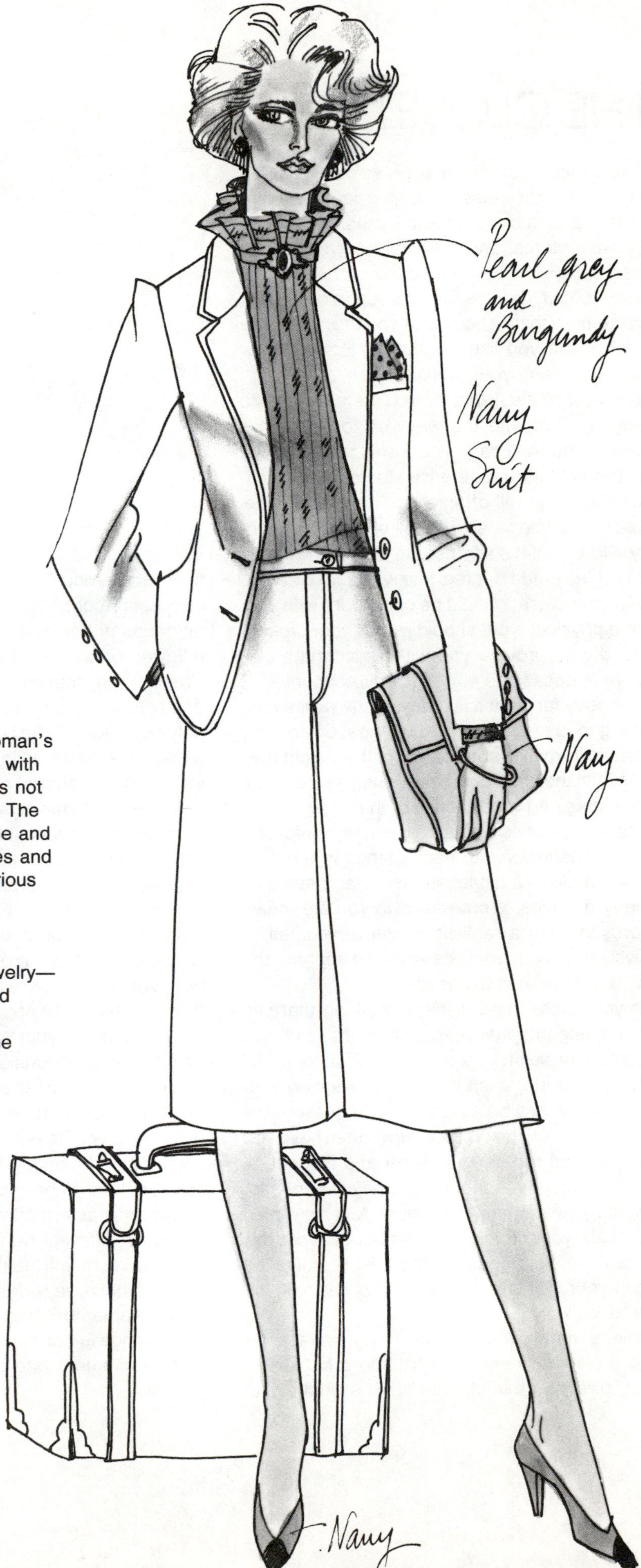

The skirted suit is the business woman's uniform. The crisply tailored blazer with a modest lapel and nice detailing is not too long or heavy to wear indoors. The straight skirt with a pleat is versatile and comfortable, but a variety of shapes and styles are available to adapt to various figure types. A flattering color and neckline are the most important elements of a suit blouse. All accessories—bags, shoes, and jewelry— are tailored, compatible in style and scale with the whole outfit, and appropriate to the personality of the wearer.

Pearl grey
and
Burgundy

Navy
Suit

Navy

Navy

5 THE CLOSET CASE

A trained psychologist can learn a great deal about a person by looking in her closet. Clothing and how it is stored tells about peoples' habits and tastes, their priorities and economic status, and their values and general concepts of sexuality. You can make the same kinds of judgments for yourself. Take a look through your closet and at the same time think about who you are. What are your goals? What are you like physically? How do your clothes fit your body and your ambitions?

Think about your goals. What do you want to change about the way you live and the way you look? Gain a sense of yourself and the image you want to project. Set your sites on the next step on the way to your ideal self-image. A radical change will often cause a person to feel uncomfortable. Your image should be evolutionary, not revolutionary. Eliza Doolittle's transformation at the hands of Professor Higgins made her feel she was a fake at first. The clothing in your closet should be consistent with your personality and physical type, should reflect your present life-style, and should provide you with appropriate garments to wear for occasions you regularly encounter.

Accept your body for what it is today. Many women are constantly trying to lose the same 10 pounds. Often, they purchase a size too small in anticipation of the weight they intend to lose. All their clothes seem snug, a constant reminder of the imagined imperfection of their figure. Tight clothes emphasize a body's lumps and bumps, reinforcing the feelings of inadequacy with each glance in a mirror. Look at yourself nude in a full-length mirror and evaluate your pluses and minuses. Work with who you are today. Live in the present with a realistic sense of yourself. A positive analysis of your figure is essential to applying the rules of design to your specific needs.

Clean out your closet and discard anything that you have not worn during the past year. Donate it to a charity for a tax donation, or sell it to a used clothing store. Old clothes clutter your mind, even if you have room in your closet for them. They may be a sign that you treasure the past more than you value the present. How often have you looked at the jammed rod in your closet and thought, "I have nothing to wear," even though you have spent a lot of money on all those clothes? You must develop a plan and use it to guide your clothing purchases to avoid this situation. Write down your goals for the next year. Define the priorities in your life. List the types of occasions you will be involved in.

For example, a woman who has been a homemaker for a decade has an entirely new set of situations to plan for if she is about to reenter the job market. She must evalu-

ate her needs and find her style. Perhaps she has not had to wear "serious" clothes for the last 10 years and is uncertain about how to pull together a wardrobe for the demands of her new life. She may have been a fashion follower, or she may have bought only clothing that was washable, inexpensive, and adequate for the needs of her domestic life. A change to a more traditional style is probably necessary if she is going to work in an office or sales situation. A basic, tailored suit would be a good starting investment. A skirted suit would be appropriate for interviews and for starting the new situation. She could then evaluate the new environment, using role models on the job. Taking the basic suit as the cornerstone of her working wardrobe, she could add pieces to go with the jacket and skirt to extend their use. Well-selected garments can cross over into informal life. The tailored jacket works well with a silky blouse and a pair of trousers for an informal occasion. Accessories change the appearance of a basic dress and make it appropriate for evening wear.

As you make your plan for your remodeled closet, remember special considerations for your particular career and location. Some professions traditionally expect a certain kind of appearance. Where you work affects the kind of clothing you select. Large cities usually demand more sophisticated clothing than small towns. The South and Midwest tend to be more conservative than the sun-belt states and eastern cities. The amount of traveling you do will place different demands on your wardrobe.

Experiment with fashion to create a desired image of yourself, but always deal with the realities of your face and figure. Remember that change is typical of life and fashion. Change is not something to resist. It is the spice that adds excitement and zest to your wardrobe as well as your life.

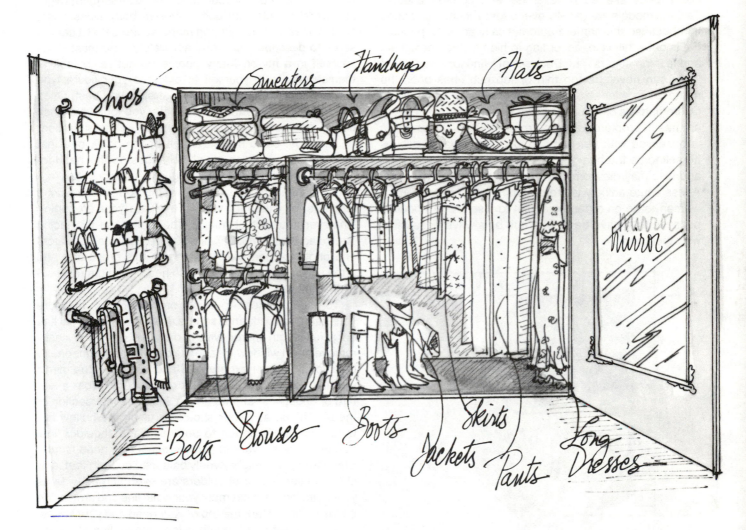

Shoes

Sweaters

Handbags

Hats

Mirror

Belts

Blouses

Boots

Skirts

Jackets

Pants

Long Dresses

Your closet should be neat, well lighted, and organized for easy selection.

6 THE BARE ESSENTIALS

Every era idealizes a different kind of woman. The modern fashion image is a tall, slender, athletic woman with an active body shaped by exercise and cottage cheese. Fashion models are usually over 5 feet 7 inches and bone thin because the camera automatically adds 10 pounds. Fat is out—thin is in, according to high fashion designers and fashion editors. The Duchess of Windsor's statement "You can never be too thin or too rich" has been the motto of fashionable women for several generations. Overemphasis on thinness has contributed to some modern health problems, like anorexia nervosa. The anorexic is obsessed with her body image. She always believes herself to be too heavy and refuses to eat. Untreated, an anorexic may die from starvation or related body stress. A less acute anxiety is more common and causes many women to be on a perpetual diet to lose 5 or 10 pounds because they have been taught to be always dissatisfied with their body.

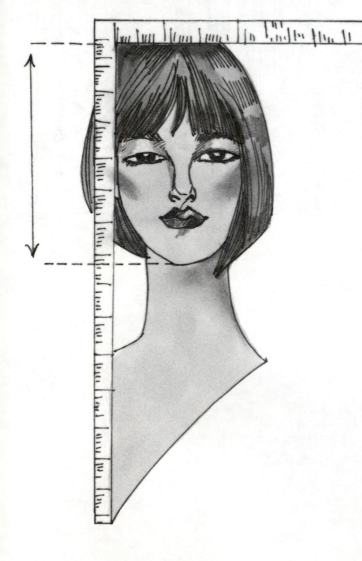

Whatever the ideal, the first step you must take in remodeling your wardrobe is to analyze your present body type. You can't go by your size. One size garment might fit several people with quite different body types. Also, sizing varies so much among manufacturers that it cannot serve to describe your body accurately. You must study yourself in a mirror. Many people do not really look at themselves. Train yourself to evaluate your figure type and learn the apparel formula that suits you best. Once you have found the tricks that make you look your best, buying clothes and dressing each day will be simplified.

The most basic measurement of the body, one that does not change with weight changes, is the head-to-height proportion. An average figure is usually between 7 and 7½ head heights tall. This method of measuring height is an important way to evaluate your proportion whatever your actual height. The sketch on the facing page diagrams a typical 7-head figure. Fashion illustrators and photographers like to elongate this proportion and often use very tall models whose head-to-height ratio is 8 or 9 lengths.

To find your head-to-height proportion, first measure your head size with an L square. Next draw a vertical line on a full-length mirror with a dark felt pen (it is easily removed with window cleaner). You will need someone to help you with the next steps. Stand in front of the mirror with the vertical line centered on your body. Wear a leotard or underwear and no shoes. Mark the intersection of the plumb line and your shoulders using the hollow between your collarbones to determine the shoulder line. Square a line for your shoulders equal to 1 head length. Stand with your weight evenly balanced on both feet, and check to see if your shoulders are even and as wide as your head length. Next mark your waist line and crotch line on the vertical. Mark the top of your head and your knees.

Measure off head lengths along the vertical. You are likely to be a little more than 7 head lengths tall. Now put on some high-heeled shoes (about 2½ to 3 inch heels) and stand next to your plumb line. You can see that your proportions have elongated so that now there are closer to 7½ head lengths to your total height.

notch
line

plumb
line

FLOOR

mark your figure proportions in red on the vertical line

7 THE BALANCED FIGURE

A balanced figure has an equal drop (difference) of 10 inches between the bust, waist, and hip measurements. A size 8 would measure (depending on the manufacturer, of course) a 36-inch bust, 26-inch waist, and 36- to 37-inch hip (measured 7 inches below the waistline). The balanced figure has a well-defined shoulder line. The ideal shoulder width is 1 head length measured from the center plumb line. Models always have wide shoulders to carry clothes and allow them to drape over a slender body. The balanced figure wears the same size top and bottom. It is the easiest body type to dress.

As a body gains weight, the weight tends to be distributed in a consistent pattern. The balanced figure would add weight equally at the bust, waist, and hips. An extremely heavy balanced figure may add more weight at the waist than the bust and hips.

Have your assistant mark the width of your shoulders on the shoulder line you have drawn across the plumb line. Mark the width of your torso at the bust, the waist, and the hips. Connect the marks to create your "mirror image." Measurements are often misleading because the flesh is distributed around the body in many ways. One person who measures 36 inches at the bust may have a small back and a full bosom, while someone else may have a wide back and a small bosom. Stand back and study your silhouette. Take circumference measurements of your bust, waist, and hips. Compare these to the silhouette drawn on the mirror. Evaluate your figure shape based on these calculations.

Factors other than measurements and distribution of weight influence the silhouette and appearance of a person. Posture is the most important of these. Helen Armstrong defines posture types in *Patternmaking for Fashion Design*.[1] A *perfect stance* aligns the earlobe, mid-shoulder, and ankle on a vertical line. The *upright stance* has an arched back which thrusts the bust and abdomen forward. High-heeled shoes that fit poorly or are too high force a person to use the upright stance for balance. Good posture can improve the figure. The perfect stance and a comfortable upright stance make a heavy figure seem more lithe and graceful. Heel height can elongate your proportions, but height at the expense of moving gracefully is a serious mistake.

The woman with a slender, balanced figure that is proportioned at 7 head heights or more can wear almost all kinds of fashions. Even the most extreme style variations will look good on her, and this is the ideal figure for which most high fashion designers create.

---

[1]*Patternmaking for Fashion Design* is an excellent reference book for the home sewer with a figure problem. It shows how to adjust patterns to accommodate size differences that occur in top-heavy and pear-shaped figures.

The crotch is usually about midway between the top of the head and the floor. Legs that are shorter in proportion to body height can be lengthened visually by garments that emphasize vertical style lines. A large head affects the head-to-height ratio and tends to make a person seem shorter.

The heavier balanced figure may look boxy and needs to emphasize the vertical to seem taller. Height balances this bulkier silhouette. A very heavy figure will make the head seem too small. A fuller, soft hairstyle helps to balance the silhouette. Hands and feet appear more delicate and are good features to focus on as more weight is added.

Transfer your silhouette to the page with a red outline if you have a balanced figure. Have an assistant evaluate your posture with high-heeled shoes and then with bare feet. How does your posture affect the total picture? Experiment with several kinds of shoes to determine the most graceful heel height that still allows for a free and easy stride.

If you have a balanced figure, use a red marker to draw your silhouette as you see it in the mirror over the center figure.

8 THE PEAR-SHAPED FIGURE

The most typical figure deviation in American women is the pear-shaped figure. This figure type has a smaller bust and waist in proportion to the size of the hips and thighs. Women who have jobs that require little movement and a great deal of sitting often settle into this shape. As this figure type gains weight, the proportion is maintained, with most of the increase going to the hips, thighs, and buttocks.

Careful dressing can conceal this figure deviation and create an illusion of slenderness because most people focus on the figure from the waist up. Clothes that focus on the face make the most of this figure type. The upper torso and waist are usually the slimmest parts and should be emphasized. Bust shape can differ even though circumference measures equally. An ideal distribution of figure fullness is when there is slightly more view of the bust than the back when seen in profile. Many pear-shaped figures have very bony necks and chests. A revealing neckline will emphasize this.

Emphasize the upper torso with light and bright colors, patterns, and horizontal lines. Horizontal stripes can be worn above the waist. Define the waistline with interesting accessories and wide belts. Soft blouses styled with gathers, bust pockets, and interesting shoulder details balance the top and bottom. Jewelry should attract the eye to the neck and hands and can be quite dramatic. The dressmaker suit with a waist-defining jacket and a slightly flared hip line over a softly gathered skirt will be flattering.

Play down the figure from the waist down. The most flattering bottom for this kind of figure is the flared skirt that fits smoothly over the hips and falls below the knees. This skirt may be patterned in a subdued print or plaid but is best in a neutral or receding color. A soft dirndl skirt with enough ease to soften the transition from the small waist to the wider hip is a good choice. Hem length depends on the shape of the legs. A flattering choice is a hem that falls at the fullest part of the calf so the visible leg is tapering to the ankle.

Pants that fit well can be flattering. A pleated waistline will minimize the curve of the hips if the figure is not too heavy. Pants should be well tailored with a crisp front crease. Avoid clinging knits and select woven fabrics. Layering a jacket or vest over pants will minimize the difference between the small torso and the full hips.

A delicate shoe and a stocking the tone of the bottom will minimize the bulges of a heavy calf. Do not wear contrasting shoes or stockings because they will draw attention downward and the eye will automatically compare the size of the hips to the size of the feet.

Avoid drop torso styles and tops that end at the hip line. Wear tops that end above the fullest part of the hip or below the crotch line. Any details that draw attention to the hips, like buttons or pockets, should be avoided.

The rear view of the bottom-heavy figure is very important. Always evaluate this figure in a three-way mirror. Make sure that jackets worn over a fitted skirt or pants cover the derriere. Pants should fit without crease lines, bulges, or stress lines. Skirts should flare from the fullest part of the figure without hemline distortion.

Block in your silhouette on the mirror-image of your figure. Transfer the silhouette shape to this page with a red outline if you fit into this figure category.

Perfect stance is when the earlobe, mid-shoulder, and ankle align on a straight vertical. Upright stance has a forward thrust of the stomach so the earlobe and the shoulder fall behind the vertical.

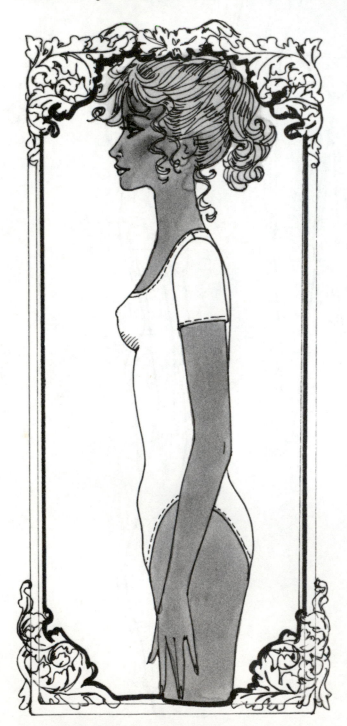

If you have a pear-shaped figure, draw your silhouette in red over the front-facing figure.

9 THE TOP-HEAVY FIGURE

A very full bust with a slender waist and hips is the second figure deviation. This figure type was the fashion ideal of the 1890s when the Gibson girl with her full bosom and slender hip line was the rage. This figure type is still the modern sex symbol, as personified by Marilyn Monroe.

This figure deviation is more difficult to conceal than the pear shape because of the prominence of the upper torso. Most women with this figure type want to dress down their bust line. They want to seem taller, because even a woman of average height seems smaller if she has a large bust.

The key to dressing the top-heavy figure is to minimize the torso by using receding colors and simple vertical details and to emphasize the hips and legs to balance the larger top. Vertical lines should not run over the bust but to the side or center front. Avoid decorations at the bust area, such as pockets or buttons. Bright colors and bold prints draw the eye to the area covered, so reserve these for bottoms. A full bust makes the torso seem shorter, so avoid any design elements, such as strong horizontals and wide belts, that further shorten the visual dimensions of the bodice.

Foundation garments are important to control the bust line. Wear a minimizer bra that has been carefully fitted to soften the bust line and contour it naturally. Make sure the straps are the right length, well balanced, and wide enough to avoid shoulder discomfort. Many women tend to round their shoulders in an effort to minimize their bust line. This posture reflects a negative body image and makes wearing clothes effectively impossible. The shoulders cease to function as hangers for the clothes. The visual length of the torso is shortened. An erect posture is extremely important for this figure type.

Layering is effective to minimize the bust. Avoid tops with a front placket that are meant to be tucked in. Select instead garments that are designed as overblouses and are long enough to create a flattering line. Belt them with a self-colored or narrow belt to lengthen the bodice visually. Vests and jackets that are worn open create a visual path that leads to the face, yet minimizes the bust area.

V-shaped necklines are flattering and direct the eye to the face. High, horizontal necklines are also good, especially when worn with a necklace that falls above the breasts in a V. Beware of wearing jewelry that falls at the fullest part of the bust. Chokers direct the eye to the face and minimize the bust. Avoid scoop necklines.

Garments that are fitted with darts and many seam lines direct attention to the full bust. They are difficult to fit correctly, and the dart or seam line leads the eye to the fullest part of the body, instead of toward the face.

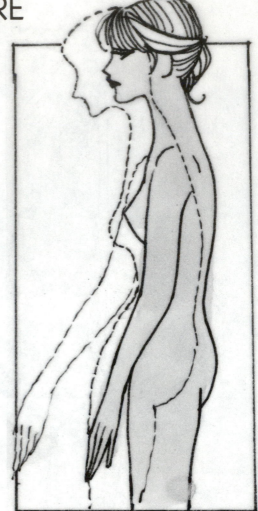

Women with a full bust line often stoop. This posture emphasizes their body characteristic.

Weight tends to collect on the upper torso as this figure type matures. Often the legs are very slender. Skirt length becomes crucial to avoid a "bird-leg" look. Skirt length will vary depending on the individual, but the most flattering length is usually two to four inches below the knee.

Flared and pleated skirts with hip detailing are flattering to this figure type. Slim skirted styles are appropriate because they give the figure a longer line. Border print skirts and contrasting shoes draw the eye to the hem away from the bust line. Softly gathered skirts and pants with fullness at the hip line (soft gathers or stitched-down pleats) balance the full bust.

Block in your silhouette on the mirror-image of your figure. Transfer the silhouette shape to this page with a red outline if you fit into this figure category.

18

If you have a top-heavy figure, draw your silhouette in red over the front-facing figure.

10 COLOR

Color surrounds and shapes our lives. Color perception depends on a human reaction to a physical phenomenon. The eye reacts to visible light wavelengths reflected from a surface. Different colors have different wavelengths. The reaction of the eye is interpreted by the brain to create the perception of color.

Seeing color is such a commonplace thing for most people that it is taken for granted. Rarely does an average person analyze how color affects life. Colors affect sensations and moods. Experience teaches humans to relate colors to feelings: crisp, sparkling, cold, pure white snow; glowing, warm, yellow-gold candle light; cool, green piny forests; dusty, beige, dry, hot deserts. Each color develops positive and negative associations.

Artists are sensitive to the link between colors and experience. They use color to express moods and sensations. Artists isolate the feeling of a color and reinterpret it graphically so others can enjoy their enhanced perception of reality.

Color creates illusions that change a physical object's appearance. Particular colors and combinations of colors can be used by fashion designers to create visual effects and to enhance the way a body looks.

Look at the simple color wheel on the facing page. Red, blue, and yellow are the primary colors. These three colors combine to create all other colors. Color them in on the wheel. Move to the next ring of colors and fill in these circles. Orange, violet, and green are the secondary colors. They are a combination of equal parts of the primary colors. The third ring of colors, tertiaries, are combinations of the adjacent colors. All the colors on this color wheel are "pure hues," or colors that have not been lightened with white or darkened with black.

Notice that part of the color wheel is labeled *cool* and the opposite side is labeled *warm*. Cool colors have a strong blue undertone, and warm colors have a yellow or red undertone. Cool colors suggest calm and serenity, while warm colors tend to be energetic and stimulating. Color-related feelings or color personalities have developed through shared, common human interaction with nature and the environment.

Black, white, and grey are not included on the color wheel. They have no hue, or wavelength, placing them in the visible light spectrum. Yet, we can see them. Black, white, and grey are true neutrals. Adding white or black to a pure color lightens it or darkens it—neutralizing the pure hue and the intensity of the wavelength it reflects. Grey is made by combining opposite colors on the color wheel in equal amounts to neutralize each individual color's light wavelength. Individual greys can have a warm or cool undertone.

A color can be cool and yet have a warm cast or warm with a cool cast. An example of this is red, which can have a blue-red cast or an orange-red cast. Both reds are warm colors, but each has a different undertone that slightly alters the color. These colors do not turn grey because the proportion of the opposite color is so small that it only tints the stronger hue. This is an important concept to understand when analyzing the colors that are most flattering to your skin tone.

Black	Charcoal	Medium Grey	Light Grey	White

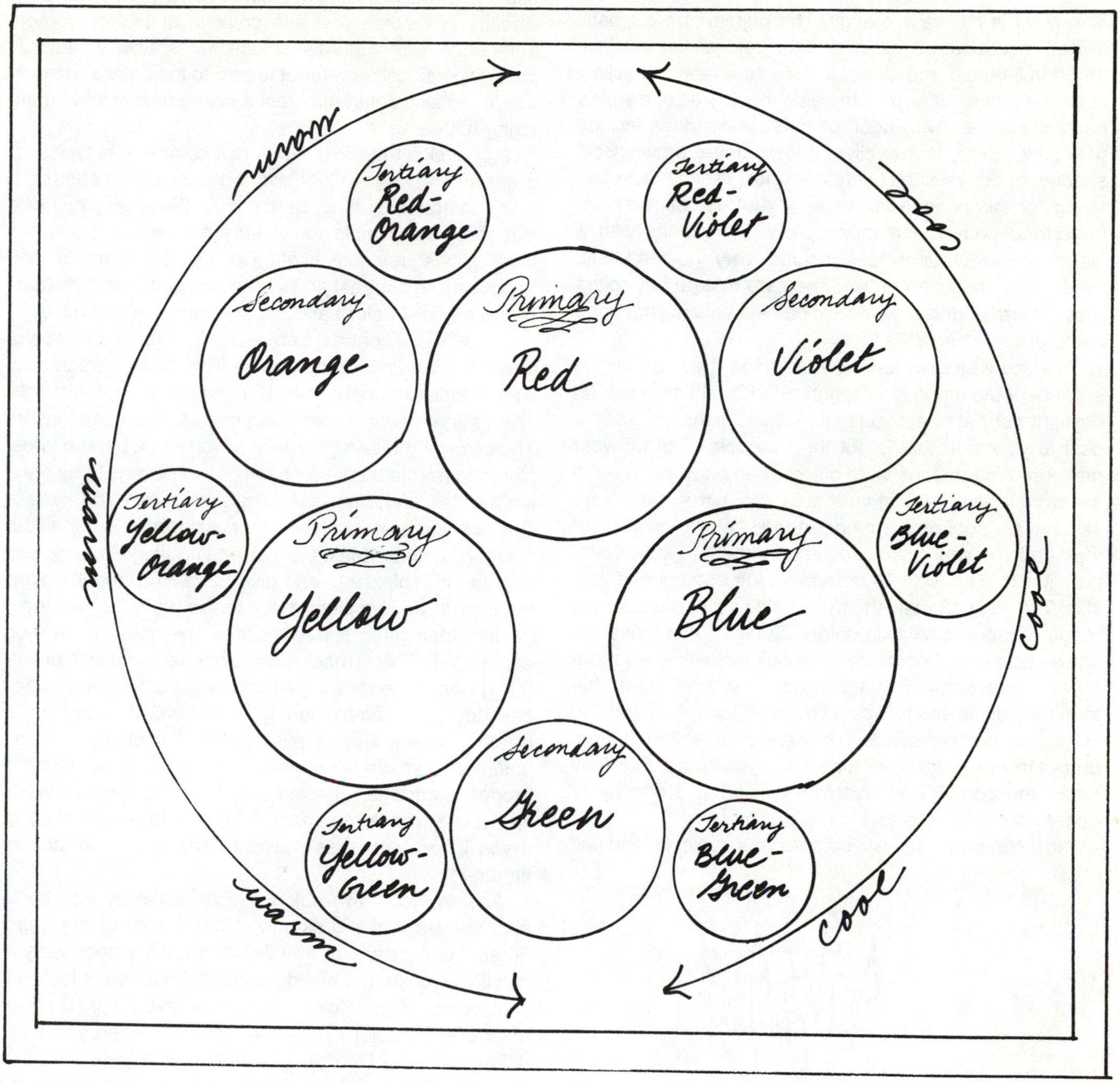
warm
Tertiary
Red-Orange
Tertiary
Red-Violet
cool
Secondary
Orange
Primary
Red
Secondary
Violet
warm
Tertiary
Yellow-Orange
Primary
Yellow
Primary
Blue
Tertiary
Blue-Violet
cool
Secondary
Green
Tertiary
Yellow-Green
Tertiary
Blue-Green
warm
cool

11 PERSONAL COLOR

Skin color is basically orange. The pigments are greatly diluted in Caucasian skins to light values and concentrated in Negroid and Oriental skins to a range of yellow to brown tones. All skin color has either a blue or a yellow cast. Skin tones with cool, or blue, undertones include pale pink, beige, taupe, olive, and charcoal brown. Cool shades, or colors with blue undertones, are the most flattering for this complexion to wear. Let us call the blue-undertone complexion *moon glow*. Skin tones with a warm, or yellow, undertone include ivory, golden beige, terra cotta, and warm brown. They are flattered by colors with a warm undertone. We will call the yellow-undertone complexion *sunlight*.

Analyze your skin tone to determine if you are in the sunlight or the moon glow range. Start by sitting in natural daylight but not direct sunlight. Artificial lights may add a cast to your skin that is not the true color. Do not wear makeup. Wear a pure white garment and a white towel to cover your hair. Look at your face in a mirror. Does your skin have a cool or warm undertone? Check the color of your body on your palms and in an untanned area. Compare it with pure white to determine the true color of your skin. The color chart on the front inside cover has a simple range of moon glow skin colors. Sunlight skin tones are shown across the top of the back inside cover. Many more tones are possible in each range of complexions, but these will guide you to typing your skin tone. Be careful in judging olive complexions. They are often sallow, but underneath the yellow overtone lies a blue cast that truly tones the complexion. Warm tones have a peachy or golden color ranging to a deep brown.

Now compare your skin color to your eye color and hair color listed as typical combinations for moon glow and sunlight complexions. Notice how hair color complements skin color to create an appropriate blending. Nature is usually correct in selecting the most pleasing combination of skin, hair color, and eye color in a healthy person. Tampering with nature's selection, especially radically changing hair colors without regard to the color and intensity of the skin color, may result in an artificial and unflattering appearance.

A cool skin tone will "fight" hair color that is typical of a warm complexion. Cool skin tones look best combined with ash brown or clear, dark colors. Silver-grey hair with a moon glow complexion is very handsome, and often moon glows grey early in life. Coloring dull or mousy hair to have more contrast and vibrancy is flattering if the cast of the artificial color balances the complexion color.

A high value contrast between skin color and hair color creates a versatile appearance. This lucky person may wear a wide range of colors. Dark hair combined with light skin or light hair with dark skin is a striking combination. The color of the skin gradually softens as a person ages. Nature corrects the loss of complexion intensity by greying the hair and often softening the color of the eyes.

Once you have analyzed your skin tone, examine your makeup colors. Makeup can camouflage blemishes, brighten complexions, and give the skin a healthy glow, but it must be complementary to the natural skin tone.

Skin tone often subtly modifies the color of makeup applied to it. This is most likely to happen, and with unflattering consequences, if you use makeup with the wrong cast for your complexion type. A sunlight complexion wearing a pink lipstick may find that it changes to an unflattering shade of dull maroon. A lipstick color with the proper undertone tends to stay "true" on the wearer's lips. It is a mistake to change lip color to match clothing if you ignore your basic palette. The effect will not be flattering.

Analyze your own coloring quite carefully and try to approximate it in the sketch at the center of the page. (Prisma pencils are an excellent tool for this because you can lightly color and blend several flesh tones to look like your complexion.) Color in your true eye color. Do your eyes change color in different lights or when you wear different colors? Dab bits of your lipstick, blush, and base at the jaw line and double-check the colors to make sure they are the right cast for you.

Moon Glow

SKIN TONES
white to delicate pink
pink-beige
beige-taupe
olive
dark brown, with
olive or blue
undertones
charcoal brown

HAIR COLORS
white
white blonde (platinum)
blue-grey
salt & pepper
medium brown
ash brown
'mousey' brown
'mousey' blonde
medium brown
black, with no
red tones

EYE COLORS
Blue: pale to deep
grey
grey-green to green
hazel & soft brown
deep brown, to
brown-black

Sunlight

SKIN TONES
ivory
peach
golden-beige
camel
soft terra cotta
warm brown
golden-brown
dark warm brown

HAIR COLORS
flaxen blonde
yellow, or golden-grey
golden-brown or
blonde
copper-red brown
auburn
red, to strawberry
blonde
red-grey
chestnut brown
deep brown-black

EYE COLORS
Brown — all shades
from golden
to hazel
amber
green
blue with yellow
undertone
blue — aqua

12 MAKEUP COLOR

Makeup, skillfully applied, will smooth the uneven color of a complexion, accent the natural contours of the face, and highlight the eyes, cheeks, and lips so they radiate a healthy glow. The best advice you can get is from a knowledgeable makeup artist who works with you to achieve a look that you are comfortable with and that enhances your appearance. Three types of color are usually applied: base color, contouring colors, and accent colors.

The base color should blend with your skin type. Foundations are formulated for moon glow and for sunlight complexions. It is essential to start with a foundation that is compatible with your basic skin coloring. Test the color on your jaw line. Cheek color is often too rosy to use as a standard for the foundation you select. Evaluate the foundation color in natural light. The lighting in a store, both incandescent and fluorescent, affects color. Be sure to look at makeup colors in daylight to avoid distortion and to be able to see the nuances of the color you are selecting. The base color you select may have to be darkened if you tan, but otherwise it is not changed. Foundation color is never changed to "match" clothes.

A foundation should even the color of your skin and cover small blemishes. Blend it well into the hairline and under the jawline so that you have a natural look. Heavy foundations tend to look artificial in daylight. Base makeup is either water-base or cream-base. A water-base foundation can be thinned and applied with a small natural sponge.

Coutouring colors are used under the cheekbones and sometimes on other parts of the face to minimize width or to accentuate bone structure. Contouring colors are made in powdered and cream form. They must be blended with the fingers, a puff, or a cotton ball so that the color seems to disappear, yet leaves the illusion of a shadow on the contours of your face. Blending is essential to achieve a smooth, natural look. Highlight contouring is often used under the eyebrow and at the very top of the cheek. Sometimes, a heavier foundation or makeup stick will be necessary to mask shadows under the eyes or dark facial blemishes. Contouring makeup does not change color to go with the clothing colors you wear.

Accent coloring is the third category of makeup. Accents include eye shadow, blush or rouge, lipstick, and mascara. Accent colors can vary with the colors you wear and will be influenced by fashion, but they must be compatible with your color type. The secret of accent coloring is to use enough color to create an aura of health that complements your clothing colors without competing with your natural shades and looking artificial.

Sunlights should wear accent makeup with an orange-apricot base. They can wear the subtle brown tones and the smokey greys when wearing cool colors. Green eye shadows are excellent for the hazel- and green-eyed sunlights. Moon glows should stick to the rose-pink family for blushers and lipsticks. Soft, greyed blues accent blue eyes when used as a shadow, but too bright a blue is startling.

Lipstick shades are most influenced by fashion trends. Very pale lipstick, lighter than your skin tone, creates a peculiar illusion even if it is fashionable. Dark or very bright lipstick can sometimes produce unnatural effects that are harsh and unflattering. Bright or dark lip color works best with a dramatic garment worn by a person with high contrast coloring.

The more makeup contrasts with skin, the more artificial it will look. As the skin ages, makeup colors should be reevaluated to go with the softened complexion and color of the hair.

It is wise to review your goals for wearing makeup. Exaggerated artifice detracts from a person's appearance and is usually inappropriate for daytime. Very natural makeup, on the other hand, can be too light to accent the best elements of your face, especially in the evening. Strive to arrive at a happy medium. Patronize a local department store's cosmetic department or visit a beauty salon with a competent makeup artist, and allow these experts to show you how to apply cosmetics to build your skills in enhancing your best assets.

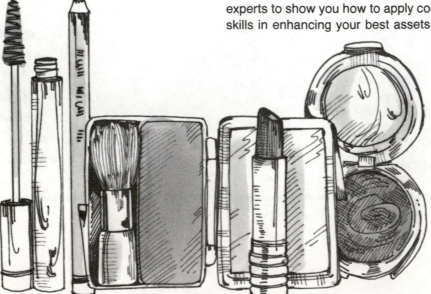

Foundation
- All over face

Toner
- darken cheekbones
- narrow jaw with toner if too wide
- highlights under eyebrow & top of cheeks

- tone eyelids & occipital bone
- blush for cheeks
- mascara
- lipstick

Test your _makeup_ colors — first at the side of the face

- Are all colors in the same palette?
- Try several different shades of lipstick to cover your entire wardrobe
- Test for compatibility

13 COLORING YOUR WARDROBE

Plan your wardrobe like a professional designer would design a line. Work with the colors for your palette that are on the front and back inside covers of this book. Begin by selecting several basic colors, called *base goods colors,* for your structured clothes (tailored garments in heavy fabric) as well as for some lightweight garments. Base goods colors are the foundation of the wardrobe, the colors that will combine with many other shades. Notice that the sunlight palettes emphasize warm basics, and the moon glow palettes contain cool neutrals, such as grey and taupe.

Now consider the fashion base goods colors. These colors shift with the seasons and fashion, but they are still the colors for the basic parts of your wardrobe. It is not important to match these colors exactly, but to use them as a key to selecting the range that is most appropriate for your coloring. Evaluate the newest colors in a fashion season in a dressing room with natural light. Wear makeup, especially the correct base. Your makeup accents can be changed to go with the newest shades, but, of course, they must remain within your palette. Select bottoms and tailored jackets from the fashion base goods colors. Stick to your base goods colors to guide your shoe purchases. A limited number of shoes and handbags in a neutral tone that blends with your basics will pull your whole color story together.

Next, branch out to the neutral blouse goods colors. Blouse goods colors are worn close to the face. They are light, neutral colors that should lighten and brighten a complexion and link your face, the base goods colors, and the more brightly colored accents. The exact shades of these blouse tones will be modified by the season, but the general range blends with all of the base goods colors in each palette and enhances skin tones. Figures that are best in light-colored bottoms can team these with rich dark colors from their palette.

Move now to the bright blouse, accessory, and dress colors. These colors can be used as whole garments, especially in dressy or casual clothes. Bright colors seem more appropriate for soft garments. The bright palette looks especially handsome in natural fibers like silk and wool and some of the soft synthetics that dye into bright, clear shades. Dress designers often select bright colors for soft clothes because they know that these clothes do not have to be as versatile as more expensive tailored garments. Soft clothes are generally worn for a shorter time and do not have to be compatible with a great variety of other clothes. Play with accent colors. Combine them with base goods and neutrals.

Bright colors are excellent accent colors that give pizzazz to the combinations of neutrals and base colors you have in your wardrobe. A conservative combination would be a cream blouse with a navy or black bottom and matching accessories. Experiment with more adventurous combinations like brown and black accented with a red belt. A blouse printed in several colors is often used by a designer to pull together two or more base goods colors. This trick is easy to copy, because you can match skirt and jacket colors to the print for a coordinated look. Watch fashion magazines for ideas for current fashionable color schemes. These combinations are what make fashion fun and interesting. You will rarely make a mistake in color selection if you select colors from your palette.

Understanding your color palette will assist you in selecting the most flattering colors for your complexion. Remember to reevaluate the intensity of the shades you wear as your complexion mellows in middle age. Usually, a lighter, softer shade of the same color will be more appropriate for the softer, mature complexion.

Some colors are not successful commercial colors. They have a limited following because they are thought of as too sophisticated or too ordinary or tend to make many complexions look sallow. Greens, especially the chartreuse family and some of the bright grass greens, are often difficult to wear. Orange has a common connotation and is rarely used for fashionable clothing. Softer shades of these colors, like peach and olive drab, have more commercial success. Yellow can be a difficult color to wear if it is too bright. Mustards make many complexions look grey or sallow. Experimentation and awareness of what makes you look best is the essence of successful color selection.

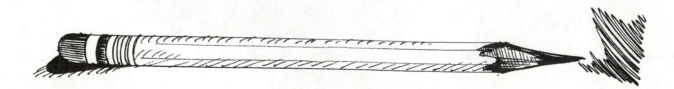

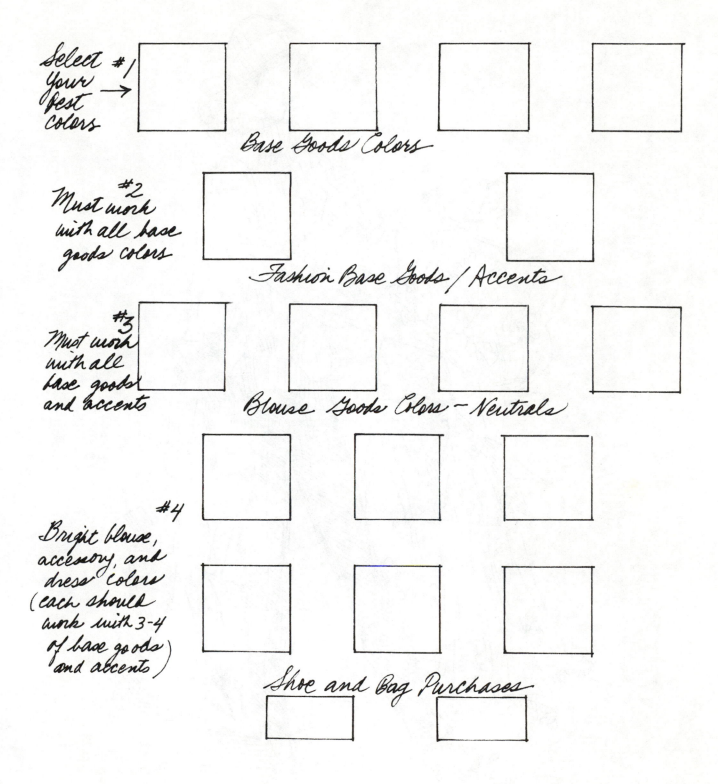

Select #1
Your
best
colors

Base Goods Colors

#2
Must work
with all base
goods colors

Fashion Base Goods / Accents

#3
Must work
with all
base goods
and accents

Blouse Goods Colors — Neutrals

#4
Bright blouse,
accessory, and
dress colors
(each should
work with 3-4
of base goods
and accents)

Shoe and Bag Purchases

14 CLOTHING SELECTION

Earlier in the book we suggested that you clean out your closet and discard your old clothes, old ideas, and old images. Now you must look critically at what you have saved and develop a plan for clothing purchases to pull together your wardrobe to suit your image and your situation. As a guide, start with the minimum basic working wardrobe for fall and spring listed later in this section. It is an outline for a working wardrobe that will take a woman through the demands of a business-oriented job efficiently. It seems larger than it actually is because all the garments can be combined to form a great variety of outfits.

We use the words *guide* and *outline* to emphasize that many variations are possible in a wardrobe. Each woman must select individual garments to fit her particular figure type and her specific life-style. A woman who works with small children at an elementary school would select the same items, but they would tend to be less formal, in brighter colors, and made from easy-care fabrics. A homemaker who is active in the community could adapt this plan, selecting fewer tailored items and adding more pieces to the suggested casual wardrobe. She could successfully use the same formula of building basic pieces into matched and coordinated suits that would carry her through her public occasions.

The sketches only suggest garment types and will be modified by fashion. Nothing dates a person more than clothes that are out of style. Subtle differences identify a suit jacket as current or one from 10 years ago. Do not be a slave to fashion, but evaluate your wardrobe seasonally or at least annually and discard pieces that are obviously from another age. While you're evaluating, remember that even classic clothes must be replaced eventually. Basic skirts and pants are worn, cleaned, and repaired so often that they simply wear out.

Lay the pieces of your wardrobe that are current and usable on the bed or the floor. Separate your spring clothes from your fall clothes. Also, put aside casual and dressy clothes and evaluate them as separate categories. You may wish to color in some of the items in the career wardrobe plans to indicate that you already have them. List the pieces that are missing from the minimum working wardrobe. Pretend you are going on an extended trip and need to pack a limited amount of garments. Pick the best of what you have and list the things you need to make the basic skirts and blouses combine in more ways as suggested by the wardrobe plans.

Armed with your list of missing pieces, swatches of your current wardrobe, and swatches of your colors (see the front and back inside covers), go shopping! An excellent rule is to buy the best garments you can afford (check the pages on construction and fit for some guidelines on how to recognize a well-constructed garment). With a limited amount of funds, buy one good garment rather than several inferior ones. Also, buy garments that you know you need to complete your wardrobe plan. In the long run, following these rules will be less expensive than purchasing many inexpensive items (complete with matching accessories) that do not last or that do not coordinate or fit into a specific wardrobe plan. European women, especially chic French women, buy one or two good outfits a season and several accessories to integrate and update the pieces already in their wardrobes. This is a way to dress well instead of having a bulging closet and "nothing to wear."

Casual and dressy additions to the basic working wardrobes are listed. These casual and dressy clothes for both spring and fall can be combined with the daytime basics for each season to cover a complete range of occasions. Clothes for active sports are not listed; they would be added to your wardrobe according to your specific interests.

Color suggestions are made for each color palette, but remember they are only suggestions to stimulate your thoughts on how to pull together a coordinated color story. These colors have been selected for an average, balanced figure. Each person should modify them according to specific figure types. For example, lighter-toned bottoms with darker tops would minimize the bust. Women who want to look taller would select more matching garments and fewer mismatched suits. Use the basic plans only as a suggestion, and then adapt them to the formula that is most flattering for your figure type. Use tracing paper to draw more pants, skirts, and blouses if you find you can start with more items in your wardrobe.

Color in your existing wardrobe and make your idealized plan even if you are not ready to go shopping. This exercise will help you eliminate costly mistakes by thinking through your purchases *before* you go to the store. Do not let a persuasive salesperson sway you from your plan. Do not purchase clothes on impulse or because they are on sale if they do not fit into your wardrobe plan.

MINIMUM BASIC WORKING WARDROBE—FALL

	Moon Glow	Sunlight
Bottoms	*Black pants Grey flannel pants *Black skirt *Burgundy skirt *Grey flannel skirt	*Black pants Camel pants *Black skirt *Raisin brown skirt *Camel skirt
Jackets	*Black suit jacket *Burgundy suit jacket Violet jacket White sweater jacket	*Black suit jacket *Raisin suit jacket Red-orange jacket Winter white sweater jacket
Tops	Grey flannel coat Pale pink, soft grey, blue-red, 　white, mauve, pale blue	Camel coat Ivory, red-orange, cream, 　camel, warm brown, buff

Accessories and dresses selected from the bright palettes

Shoes and bags in black,
　burgundy

Shoes and bags in black,
　camel

_____

*Matching garments.

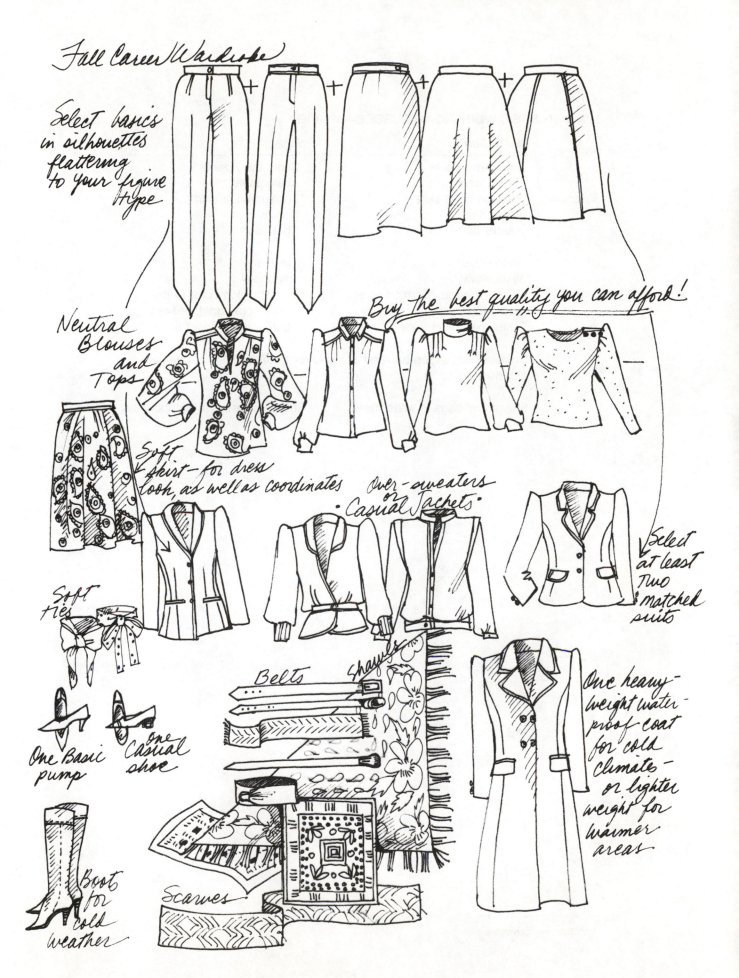

Fall Career Wardrobe

Select basics in silhouettes flattering to your figure type

Buy the best quality you can afford!

Neutral Blouses and Tops

Soft skirt — for dress look, as well as coordinates

Over-sweaters or Casual Jackets

Select at least two matched suits

Soft ties

One Basic pump

One Casual shoe

Belts

Shawls

Boot for cold weather

Scarves

One heavy-weight water-proof coat for cold climates — or lighter weight for warmer areas

MINIMUM BASIC WORKING WARDROBE—SPRING

	Moon Glow	*Sunlight*
Bottoms	Dark navy pants Taupe pants *Fashion color skirt White skirt Taupe skirt	Bright navy pants Khaki pants *Fashion color skirt Ivory skirt Khaki skirt

Tops	White blazer
	White shawl
	White, blue-red, *fashion color
	   to match skirt, sky blue
	   blue-red, plum, pink
		Ivory blazer
		Ivory shawl
		Ivory, *fashion color to match
		   skirt, coral, gold, red-orange,
		   buff, cream, bright navy

Dresses, soft separates, and accessories from the fashion palette and neutrals

Shoes and bags in white, navy	Shoes and bags in natural, navy

_____

*Matching garments.

Spring Career Wardrobe

Basic silhouette – softer shapes for very warm weather

Casual cool tops to wear under jacket for evening

Simple, neutral blazer

soft, light-weight shawl

Two pairs of blending shoes

Belts

Soft, light weight tailored dresses

CASUAL ADDITIONS TO COMPLETE WARDROBE—FALL

	Moon Glow	Sunlight
Bottoms	Jeans *Grey corduroy pants Denim or corduroy skirt	Jeans *Brown corduroy pants Denim or corduroy skirt
Jackets	Burgundy flannel jacket White wool sweater Novelty fashion color sweater (such as burgundy)	Red flannel jacket Natural wool sweater Novelty fashion color sweater (such as red)
Tops	White, blue-red, burgundy, *grey to match pants, fashion brights	Ivory, red, gold, turquoise, natural, camel, *brown to match pants, fashion brights
	Boots or casual shoes in burgundy or navy	Boots or casual shoes in cordovan or camel

CASUAL ADDITIONS TO COMPLETE WARDROBE—SPRING

	Moon Glow	Sunlight
Bottoms	Denim jeans Navy shorts Navy short skirt	Denim jeans Khaki shorts Khaki short skirt
Jackets	Lightweight navy, denim, or bright neutral jacket	Lightweight khaki or bright neutral jacket
Tops	White cotton sweater Bright neutral sweater (burgundy or pink) White, pearl grey, blue-red, chambray blue and pink, fashion brights (such as hot pink)	Natural cotton sweater Bright neutral sweater (red or royal) Buff, red, cream, plaids in warm shades, fashion brights (such as turquoise)
	Casual shoe in navy or burgundy (carry over to fall)	Casual shoes in cordovan or carmel (carry over to fall)

---

*Matching garments.

Casual Additions to Career Wardrobe

Fall
warm, thin knits
& casual
shirts

Jeans year-round

+

warm, wool sweaters

warm, outerwear
jacket

Boots
or
casual
shoes

Jeans or cotton blend
pants

Spring
casual shirts

Shorts

Skirts

lightweight sweaters

lightweight
jacket

Casual
additions
to complete
wardrobe

Plan the color scheme for dressy clothes like a small travel wardrobe based on fashion colors that are appropriate for your color type. The most recurrent neutrals in dressy garments are white and black. These colors are appropriate for all seasons. Evening clothes look elegant in jewel-tone brights selected from your color palette. Evening is a good time to wear more daring colors and prints.

For fall three basic bottoms and several dressy tops can be adapted for almost any occasion you will encounter. Select a dressy blouse that is quite covered and will blend with the neutral color of the long and short skirts and dressy pants. A useful addition is a bare top, if you can leave your arms uncovered, or a semitransparent blouse, if you prefer not to bare your arms. Cover your evening separates with a short, dressy jacket or sweater (it will go with all lengths of bottoms). An elegant silk or fluffy mohair shawl will give you added versatility. These dressy tops can be worn under a solid suit and accessorized with dressy belts and shoes for restaurant dressing.

Purchase accessories that are appropriate for both spring and fall dressy clothes if your finances are limited. One pair of dressy sandals in a dark neutral or skin tone will cover both seasons. A small evening handbag, also in a dark or neutral tone, will round out the outfits. Several bright, dressy belts or sashes will accent your waist and change the look of the separates.

Spring separates are usually barer. Prints look casual and are a natural for spring and summer. Your shawl from the fall selection can double as a cover-up for your summer outfits if you plan carefully.

Add dresses and additional soft pieces in both categories if finances permit. These selections are a basic formula for a minimum wardrobe. Try out your coordinating skills by coloring in the dressy wardrobe in colors that are versatile and suited to your personality and complexion.

Dressy Accessories

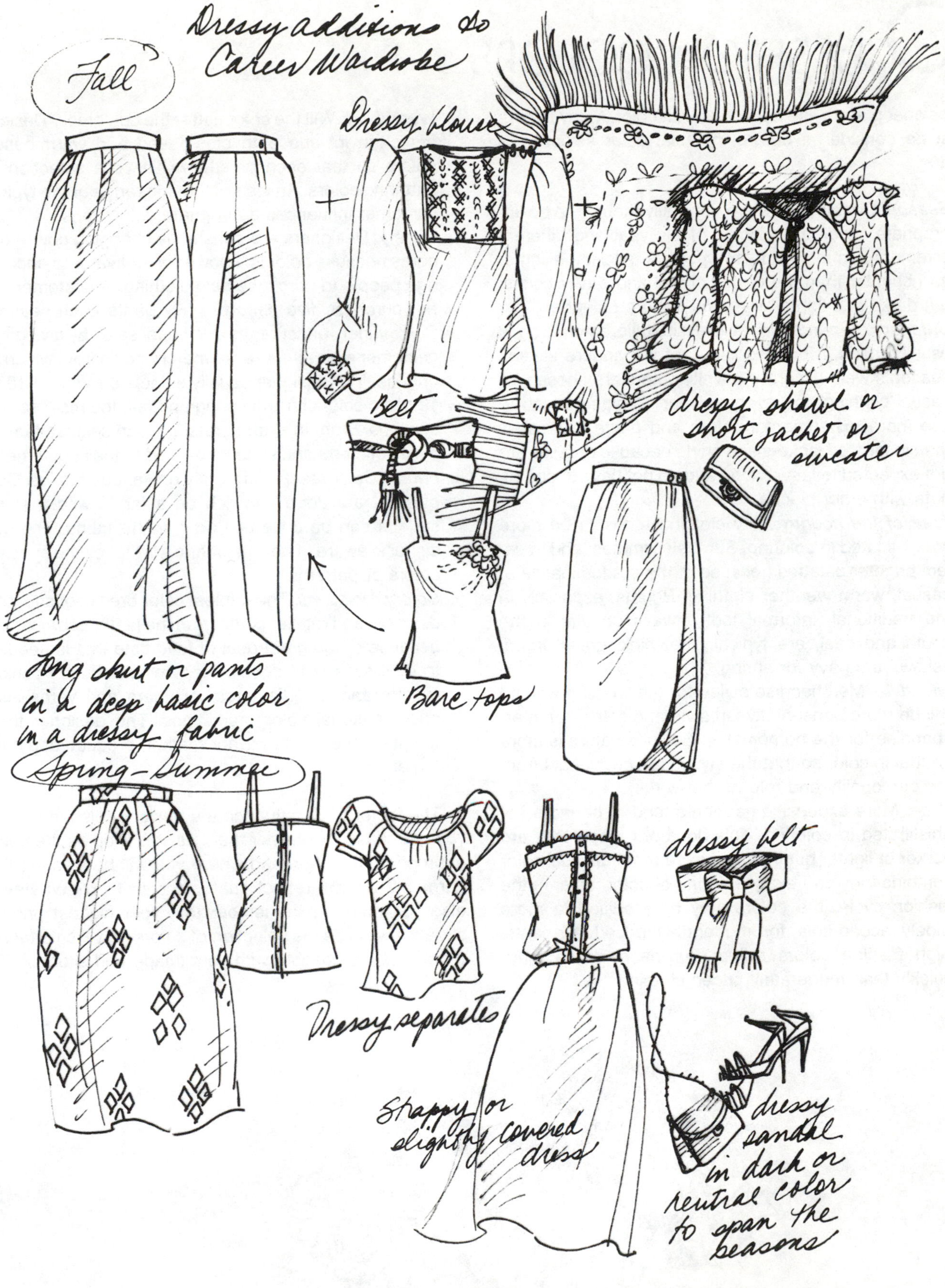

Dressy additions to
Career Wardrobe

Fall

Dressy blouse

Belt

Bare tops

Long skirt or pants
in a deep basic color
in a dressy fabric

dressy shawl or
short jacket or
sweater

Spring-Summer

Dressy separates

dressy belt

Strappy or
slightly covered
dress

dressy
sandal
in dark or
neutral color
to span the
seasons

15 FASHION COLORS

A designer plans a line beginning with color. Many factors must be considered before the final color selection is made.

1. *Season.* Certain colors are generally thought to be appropriate for different times of the year and different climates. Summer and spring colors tend to be lighter and brighter than the dark, rich fall and winter colors, but darks and lights are found in both palettes.

2. *Category of merchandise.* Classic, tailored clothing is usually made in basic colors that will endure several season's wear. Brighter novelty colors are chosen for casual clothing and evening wear. Designers tend to use more experimental colors and prints in dresses than in tailored jackets and shirts because dresses are not expected to last as long and do not have to coordinate with other pieces.

3. *Area of the country.* City clothing tends to be more sophisticated in coloring. Sun-belt climates tend to select brighter palettes because of the predominance of casual, warm weather clothing. Brights, especially in the traditional, informal look always popular in the south and east, are typically hot pink, grass green, yellow, and navy for spring.

4. *Life-style.* Merchandise styled for the working woman will be more conservative in style and color than merchandise for the homemaker. Business attire is more neutral in color so that the style does not detract from the personality and role of the worker.

5. *Price.* More expensive garments tend to be more sophisticated in coloring. This does not mean they are darker or lighter but that they have more unusual color combinations and exaggerations of color. Later in the fashion cycle, the colors may be modified to more widely acceptable for moderately priced garments. High fashion colors reflect European trends more quickly than moderately priced clothing.

6. *Wearability.* Will the color flatter the customer? Designers often include both blue-based and warm-based colors so that each palette will have a selection of flattering colors. An idea of the age range of the typical customer influences appropriate colorations.

7. *Variety.* Designers are constantly changing color concepts because color is a powerful motivator to encourage people to purchase new clothing. A customer will not purchase five pairs of navy pants each season. Color variety encourages additional sales by giving the customer a greater array of merchandise from which to choose. The designer usually selects a range of 10 to 12 basic colors for the spring and fall, the main selling seasons. From this range retailers can select different mixes of merchandise to be offered to their customers.

8. *Fabric.* Color reacts differently on various fabrics. Colors that are deep and rich on a fabric with a shiny surface can be quite dull on a matte fabric. The designer is aware of how the fabric will "take" the specific colors or patterns.

9. *Color predictions.* The earliest color predictions for the designer and retailer come from the leather companies because of the great deal of lead time that is needed to dye, style, and develop leather products. Fashion reports and manufacturers of fibers and yarns also offer seasonal color predictions. The designer then adapts these colors for her market, product, and customer.

The factors that influence the designer also influence your purchases. Consider them as you shop. Is the color appropriate for when and where you will be wearing the garment? Does it reflect quality and fashion? Whatever else you consider, remember that your highest priority should always be the selection of colors that are flattering to you and compatible with your image and situation.

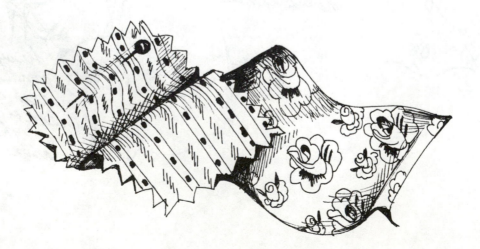

Colors in my Wardrobe

BLOUSES

SWEATERS

COAT

JACKET

PANTS, SKIRTS, SUITS

BRIGHTS

NEUTRAL RANGE - LIGHTS

My Best Colors

BASICS

Use 3"x5" file cards—cut tiny swatches out of the seams of your existing wardrobe, and tape, pin, or staple to card. Use card to select prints and additional pieces for your wardrobe. Make another card with swatches of your most flattering colors. Do not look for exact matches. Use card to select the color range best suited for you.

Sunlight

COLOR PROFILES

Colors affect people differently. Even though there are shared feelings about what colors mean, an individual's reaction to a color will be changed by past experiences. For example, being complimented when she wears a particular red sweater will register as a pleasant experience and cause a person to wear that sweater more often and to purchase more garments in that color. A person may tire of a color or connect it with an unpleasant situation and avoid the shade even though it is flattering.

Environment, life-style, and personality condition people to like specific colors. A person who wants to avoid attention and confrontation would not be likely to select bright, advancing colors, even if they made her more beautiful. A person raised in an exuberant family in a warm, casual environment might find it difficult to conform to the somber greys and neutrals that dominate business apparel.

People develop clothing personalities, that is, they adopt a particular kind of apparel or a limited range of colors which may, in face, be less flattering than others. The traditionalist, for example, has a limited palette for casual clothing and a narrow range of navy, grey, and taupe for "serious" clothes. Breaking out of the usual clothing type is difficult.

Knowing your physical color type and working with the range of colors that looks best with your complexion and hair color is the first step toward selecting the best color environment for you, both in apparel and living space. Understanding your color personality and why you prefer certain colors is the second step. Knowing yourself is often difficult, but try to define your personality type and recognize your desire to blend in with the crowd or to stand out. Remember that the sunlight and moon glow colors are suggesting a *range* of colors that will flatter your skin, but they are not the only colors that are flattering. You should experiment to find your own unique blend of colors, personality, and look.

A third step toward finding a suitable color environment is understanding the characteristics that colors have, quite apart from your physical type or personality type. Colors have unique personalities, with positive and negative aspects. These personalities may be particularly important in your preference for them.

moon glow

16 RED

Red is the first color a baby responds to. It is a warm, romantic, sensual, aggressive color. Red rooms make food look very appealing and encourage eating. Red increases a person's pulse and awareness of surroundings. Red's positive associations include Christmas and Valentine's Day. The negative aspects of red center on its associations with heat and the devil.

Men tend to respond most favorably to a yellow-based red; blue-based reds tend to attract women's attention first. Red in apparel or an interior reflects in a person's complexion. Because rosy cheeks are associated with health, the red reflections may make a person seem healthy, but they also may make an already flushed complexion look too florid or may overwhelm a pale, pink skin.

Red is an advancing color, a color to be noticed. It is often worn by positive, extroverted personalities. In an outfit it will focus attention on the part of the body it covers. In its large range of shades and tones, it can blend with many other colors and act as a bright neutral. It is used in both men's wear and women's wear.

Fire-Engine Red

Scarlet

Cranberry

Charcoal grey

Black

Burgundy

43

17 PINK

Pink is a unique color, not just a softer version of red. Pink is a feminine color. It is associated with a delicate, nonagressive, yet pleasing personality. When associated with products or food as a packaging, it appears to enhance the way a thing performs or tastes. The bakery boxes colored in soft pink make us anticipate the delicious cake we know is inside.

A mid-tone pink called *Baker-Miller pink,* after the doctors that discovered its calming attributes, actually subdues a person's actions for a limited time. This color physically inhibits the secretion of adrenaline. Being placed in a Baker-Miller pink room seems to calm people suffering from anxiety or hyperactivity as if they were chemically sedated. Pink has been the traditional nursery color for girls—perhaps causing their more passive personalities to predominate.

Pink tends to be blue-based and is flattering to most moon glow skins. Worn with somber greys and authoritative navy, it flatters and softens business apparel. Sunlight complexions should wear pinks with a yellow cast, such as watermelon shades with their warm undertone.

white

Pale
Pink
and
white

White

White

White

White

Hot!
Pink

Mauve
and
White

45

18 ORANGE

Orange tends to be a "second-class" color, liked by the masses. Orange also inspires activity. These two personality traits make orange a favorite color for uniforms and for interiors of fast food restaurants that want to attract everyone, yet serve them rapidly.

Orange is sometimes used in casual clothing but is not a tremendously popular seller. Positive associations with warmth and sunsets do not enhance its overall popularity. Perhaps full-strength orange "fights" the diluted orange of Caucasian skin tones. Red-oranges are handsome on sunlight complexions and dark brown skins.

Softened, orange turns into peach, apricot, and coral. Men like to see these colors on women. The colors have an elegant feeling that is light and feminine but somehow not as frivolous as pink. They are effective, sophisticated, yet flattering backgrounds for intimate apparel and intimate rooms like bedrooms and bathrooms. These colors softly enhance the natural warmth of sunlight complexions and so are particularly flattering. They are excellent makeup and apparel colors. Moon glow complexions wear these tones with some difficulty, but the more they are softened with white, the more versatile they become.

Deepened and toned down with brown into rust and terra cotta, orange has a practical appeal for apparel, especially for fall clothing. This should be the choice of sunlight complexions. (The fall alternative for moon glows would be the burgundy-grape family, equally popular as a fall color.)

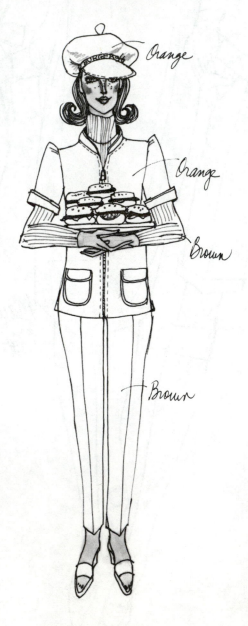

Orange

Orange

Brown

Brown

Dark Brown

Rust, Camel
and
Dark Brown

Dark Brown

Rust

Peach

Dark Brown

47

19 BROWN

Brown is a no-nonsense color, the perfect foil for sturdy country clothes in the many shades of camel through chocolate. Brown is a sincere and popular color for men, though it tends to be more casual than grey, navy, and black and therefore is worn less for serious business apparel. Browns in tweeds and suiting textures are borrowed from men's wear and are appropriate for tailored city garments and business wardrobes.

The other side of the brown personality is that it appears dirty and dull. Eastern Europeans still connect brown with the oppressive uniforms of the Nazis. This negative association has been passed down to generations who never experienced the Nazi domination.

Brown softened, develops two shades—taupe and camel—that make it appropriate for both moon glow and sunlight complexions. Taupes, or greyed browns, flatter the moon glow complexion. Taupes are neutrals that combine with many brilliant colors and are equally popular during summer and fall. Camel flatters sunlight complexions. It combines with red, cream, black, and deep brown to create rich, easy-to-live-with outfits that have a casual feeling. Combined with grey, taupes and camels are an elegant business color scheme.

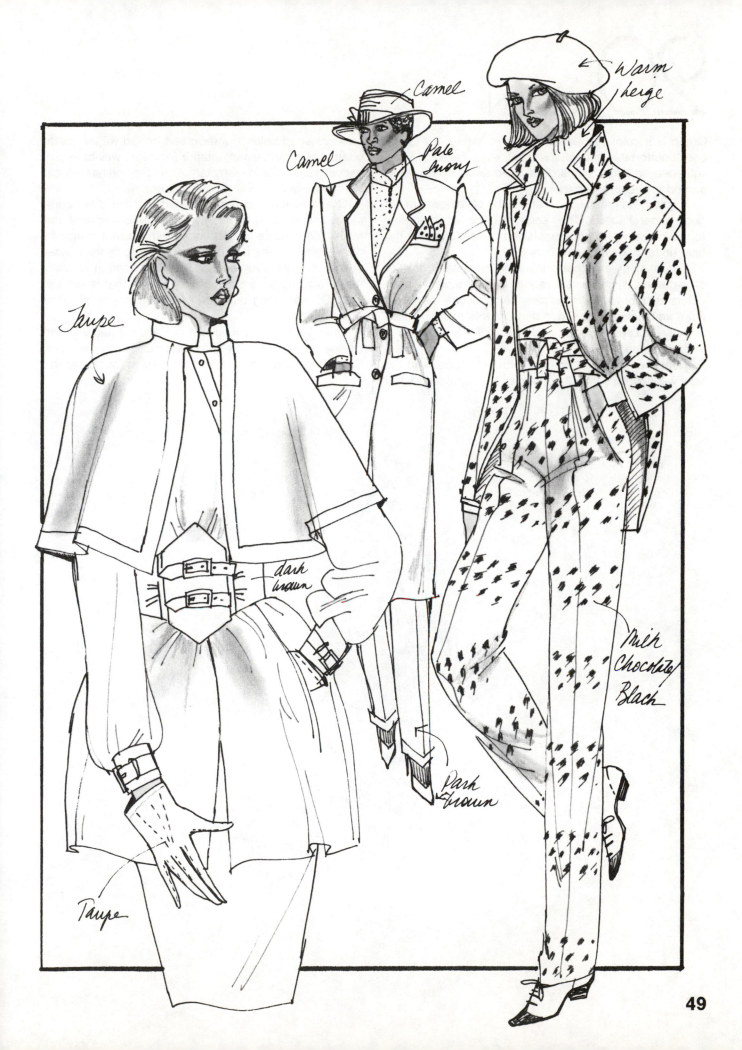

Taupe

Camel

Camel

Pale Ivory

Warm beige

dark brown

Taupe

Dark brown

Milk Chocolate/ Black

49

20 GREEN

Green is a color that surrounds us in nature and has a cool, comfortable appeal. It is a calm, neutral color when lightened and dulled. It is often used as a neutral background for hospital rooms.

Bright grass greens and many of the olive hues are not good apparel sellers. They seem to bring out the sallow tones in many sunlight complexions and clash with the blue undertones of moon glows.

Tones of greens that retail well for apparel are the blue-greens, such as teal, aqua, and turquoise. These colors are more flattering to most complexions. Turquoise is an advancing, cool shade that accents many neutrals effectively. Dresses, tops, and sweaters are often styled in these upbeat colors.

Hunter or forest green is a color that appeals to the very wealthy; less than 3 percent of the population lists it as a preferred color. Hunter green, mixed with white, is often used in an elegant interior for clean, well-bred elegance. It is a color in many tartan shades and has appeal for people with English-Scottish ancestry.

Green neutralized and softened to olive drab, commonly called *OD* in the fashion industry, is a neutral that rivals beige and camel. The ease with which it combines with brights makes it a more versatile color than other shades of green. Although it is widely used, it is really most flattering on a sunlight complexion that is not too pale. OD can bring out the sallow undertones of many complexions.

Olive green is a reminder of war and is often adapted by the very young as they fantasize about warfare. Camouflage patterns are often in fashion for teenagers.

Teal

white

Forest green

Khaki

Red Band

Forest green

Olive Drat.

21 BLUE

Blue is the preference of most people after they leave childhood. Navy blue has authority and dignity. Navy and white remind us of crisp nautical clothing. The uniforms in the navy and many police forces lend dignity to the color.

"Cardiac blue," a soft shade, is used in hospital rooms in intensive care wards because it has a calming effect. It is a natural tranquilizer but not the physical depressant that Baker-Miller pink is.

Blue is usually not associated with eating, because it is not a natural food color and does not enhance the color of red meats and foods. The most positive food association is with the crisp cleanliness of a traditional blue and white Scandinavian kitchen. Few successful restaurants are blue.

This cool, versatile color is the predominant shade of society's apparel. This is especially true of the blue "Mao suit" found in mainland China, but a look out over a crowd of westerners will prove that blue dominates their color palette also.

Navy is one of the most versatile neutral-darks. The moonglow complexion can wear inky, dark navy. Sunlights should select a clear, bright navy to wear close to the face.

Denim blue, in all its variations, has done a great deal to change western society into a blue-based apparel society. Blues in many shades, from the warm cobalts and turquoises that flatter sunlight complexions to the greyed blues that are so appropriate for moon glow complexions, are used repeatedly in fashion apparel and interiors.

Denim

Cobalt

Black

Red

White
Navy

Cream

Permissible

Hot
Pink

Cream

White

Cobalt

Permissible

53

22 PURPLE

Purple is a color that suggested wealth and royalty in the past because it was a very expensive color to produce from natural dyes.

Purple is a difficult color to combine with other colors. It is more popular with women than men. It remains an exotic color that is used sparingly in fashion, although it does have specific fashion cycles and is sometimes very popular. Purple is a good color for people with deep brown skins. A warm red-violet is handsome in contrast with a sunlight brown skin. A blue-purple is effective on a moon glow brown skin.

Lavender, purple lightened with white, has the connotation of delicate old age.

Orchid is a red-based, light purple that is rejected by many people because it does not combine well with many skin tones. Orchid can increase feelings of illness and nausea.

white

Blue-
Violet

Red

Pearl
Grey

Blue-
Violet

Lavender
and
White

Hot
Pink

Hot Pink,
Pearl Grey
and
Violet Stripes

23 YELLOW

Yellow is the first color to be processed by the eye because of the length and intensity of its color waves, and so it is highly visible. When used in small amounts in dark prints, it makes them "pop" or seem more lively. Bright yellow is often used for high visibility clothing, like sailing wear (so someone washed overboard could be easily spotted) and for workers on highways.

Yellow is the most schizophrenic color in the palette. On the positive side, it seems sunny, clean, and fresh. As the dominant color of an outfit or environment, it is much more negative. It tends to create anxiety and encourage negative responses. It inhibits minor muscle movement, and persons tend to lose control of their temper more readily in yellow surroundings. The teachers and parents in a local nursery school were very proud of the sunny yellow paint job they gave the classrooms until the children moved in. The children quarreled more and often burst into tears. The anxiety level of the youngsters was greatly reduced and harmony was restored when the rooms were repainted a soft blue.

Time tends to pass more slowly in a yellow room. Imagine looking over the hood of a yellow car while you are stuck in traffic. It could be a traumatic experience, especially if you return home to a yellow kitchen!

Yellow and black is a warning-color combination. Because of yellow's high visibility, signs warning of detours or road work are yellow and black. This color combination also occurs in nature as a warning. It declares the stinging potential of bees, wasps, and yellow jackets.

Yellows are more flattering to sunlight complexions than to moon glow tones, but they should always be carefully evaluated before being worn next to the face. The yellows are effective as accents but are often unflattering as a total outfit. Yellow is successful as a bathing suit color. The bright range contrasts nicely with brown skin and enhances a tan.

Yellow retains its physical impact even when diluted with black or white. Mustards tend to make complexions look very sallow and are generally unflattering to both sunlight and moon glow color types.

Yellow and Black

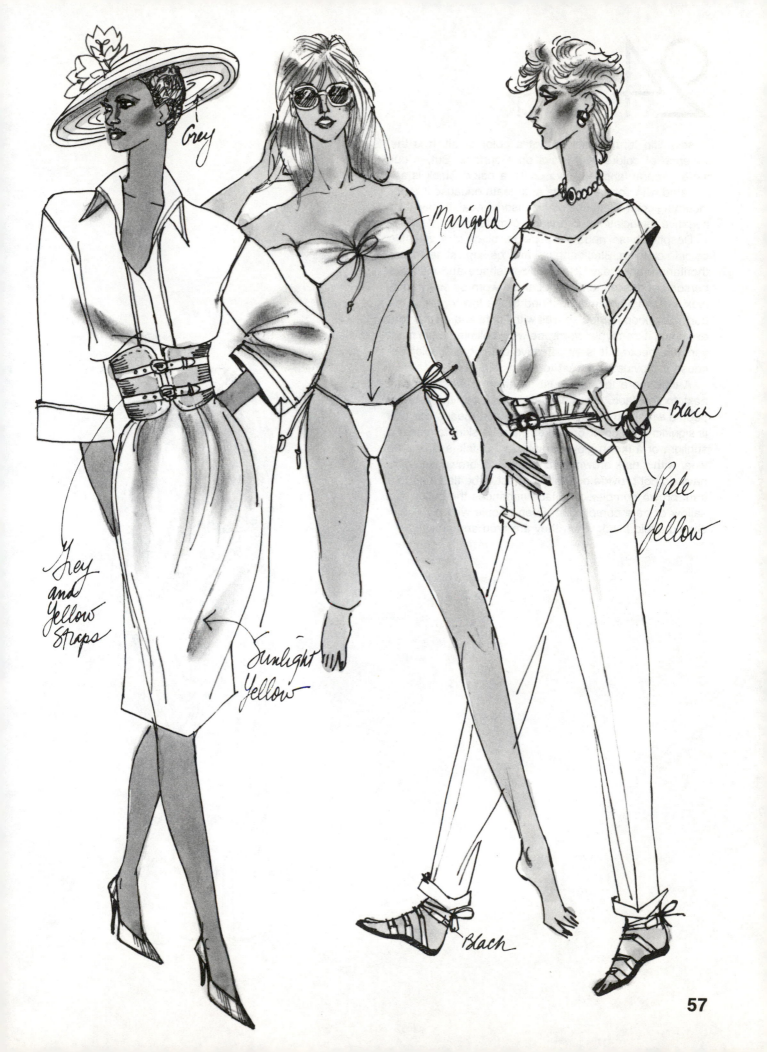

Grey

Marigold

Grey
and
Yellow
Straps

Sunlight
Yellow

Black

Pale
Yellow

Black

57

24 BLACK

In scientific terms black is not a color at all. It is the absence of colored light rays on a surface. But, in our more general language, we call it a color. Black is associated with somber events and death because it is our mourning color. Because black absorbs heat, it may have negative associations in a warm climate.

Despite these negative aspects, black is a versatile color in clothing. Black apparel may be sophisticated, authoritarian, and sexy. It neutralizes shape and makes a person seem slimmer. Black can be worn by every complexion tone when it is confined to the lower part of the body. Black combines so well with lights and brights that excluding it from your wardrobe would eliminate the most versatile neutral. It is an effective bathing suit color because it provides contrast to a tan skin.

A little more thought must be given to wearing black next to the face. Black is best worn near the face by people with high contrast. High contrast means hair that is significantly lighter or darker than the skin, for either a sunlight or a moon glow complexion. Black is difficult to wear with a dark brown skin. Black, dark brown, and dark navy do not provide enough contrast to be flattering to a dark brown complexion. Black enhances the pallor of a sallow or pale complexion. Even people with high color should avoid black when they are tired and drawn.

Black

Hot
Pink

Black
and
White
Print

Black

Hot
Pink

Black

Black

25 GREY

Grey is a sophisticated neutral that has businesslike authority. Grey is a neutral shade that neither advances or retreats and has an anonymity that makes it a natural to wear for business apparel. Clothing should form a background for the talent and expertise of business people, and the "grey flannel suit" has become the uniform of the successful business man.

Grey can be worn by both sunlights and moon glows, but it is most becoming on a moon glow complexion because it blends with and enhances the blue undertone. Soft pinks and blues combine well with grey to enhance a moon glow complexion.

Sunlights should select a charcoal grey or one with warm undertones (such as a light, greenish grey). These greys combined with cream or ivory blouses and accented with red-orange accessories make a handsome sunlight business outfit.

Fashion often uses grey, black, and white as a sophisticated combination of neutrals. Such a combination demands more dramatic and deeper rouge, lipstick, and eye shadow colors to avoid being neutralized by these sophisticated colors.

Grey

Grey and Red
Print

Black

Grey

Black

Grey
Tweed
with
Red and
Black
Flecks

Grey
Flannel

Pale Grey
and
White

Black
and
Pale
Grey
Stripe

Black

Black

61

26 WHITE

White is also technically a noncolor. When light containing all the wavelengths of the visible spectrum falls on a surface with no pigment, all the wavelengths are reflected and the eye sees white. White can seem pure and virginal (the classic wedding dress), cold and sterile, or neutral.

White has many shades and personalities. It can reflect minute shades of other colors while still seeming white and is therefore a perfect neutral. Look in a paint store at the great variety of white tones offered. These are designed to go with many different color types and tones of interior fabrics and wall coverings. Large expanses of pure white seem sterile and are usually tinted for interiors. Learn from this when selecting your apparel. White flatters the face because it reflects a pure light and is a contrast to the warm shades of the complexion. White directs the eye to the face and highlights it. This characteristic, combined with the ability of white to work with almost the entire range of colors, makes it the most versatile neutral.

Sunlights and moon glows can both wear white, in one of its tinted versions, very successfully. Creamy, warm tones are best on the sunlight complexions. Ivory is the best white next to a sunlight's face. A slight peachy undertone will flatter a yellow complexion. Blue-based whites and pure white are effective on moon glows. A hint of pink flatters the cool complexion.

White can seem frivolous and casual or elegant and dramatic for evening and formal wear. It is an excellent swim wear color in an opaque fabric because it provides high contrast to a tan skin. White reflects heat and is the classic summertime color.

Wedding White

White/
Navy
blue

White

Ivory

Marigold

Cream

63

27 COLOR ILLUSIONS

Professional apparel designers use many color illusions to create special effects in garments. They may sometimes combine colors without conscious thought about how the resulting color illusions create a beautiful garment, but more often they are applying what they know about how color works. Most professional designers evaluate a successful garment to understand what exactly was created so they can repeat their successes in the future. They have learned what effect different color combinations will have. Some of the most common of the color illusions that apply to apparel design follow.

1. *Light values advance and seem larger; dark values recede and reduce.* It is important to remember this illusion, especially when combining colors in an outfit. Dark, subdued colors are used on a part of the body that the designer wishes to minimize. A person with large hips and thighs and a small bust would dress to camouflage this problem in dark pants or a skirt and a light blouse. A dark top and a light bottom can be worn to camouflage a full bust.

This color illusion is the basis for dressing large women in black and somber colors. Unfortunately, the dark colors used to minimize bulk are often depressing and not becoming when worn near the face. However, the dark color need not be unflattering. Deep, jewel tones instead of black and somber colors will create the same illusion and give a more flattering look.

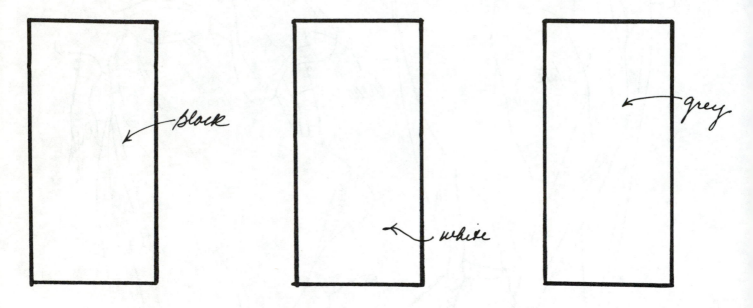

Which rectangle looks the largest?

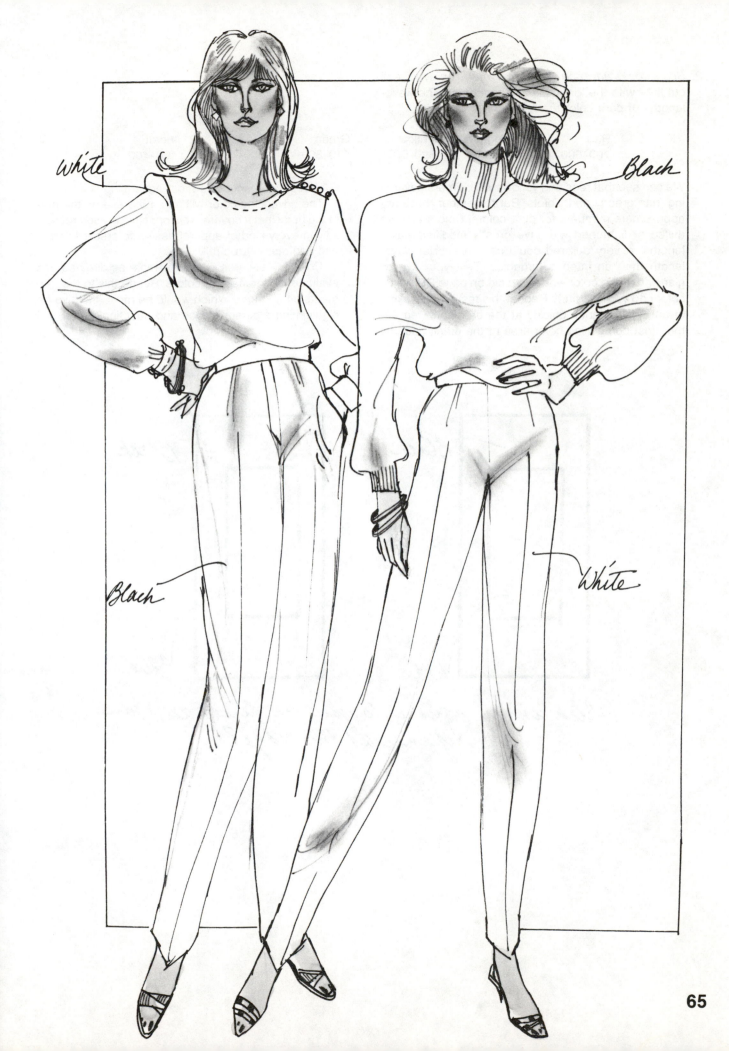

White

Black

Black

White

65

2. *Bright colors advance and seem larger.* The eye seeks out light with the longest wavelength first. The wavelengths of pure color are rated:

Red	Orange	Yellow	Green	Blue	Violet
700–600	610–590	590–570	570–500	500–460	460–400

We can see that reds and yellows will be more advancing than greens and violets. But remember these are approximate numbers for pure colors. Colors that are dulled or lightened will have greatly modified wavelengths. A very dull red could have a shorter wavelength than an intense turquoise. Test your eye by glancing at the color wheel you did on page 21. Which colors do you see first? Repeat this test when looking at an outfit. Glance quickly at the garments, register the most compelling color area of the outfit, and you will have determined the most advancing color.

The advancing color will focus the eye on the part of the body that it covers. This principle is used repeatedly in every kind of apparel design to create interest and contrast in an outfit.

Color the squares in the example as directed and evaluate the intensity of colors. Relate this to the garments on the right. Which would be most effective for highlighting a person's face and bust line?

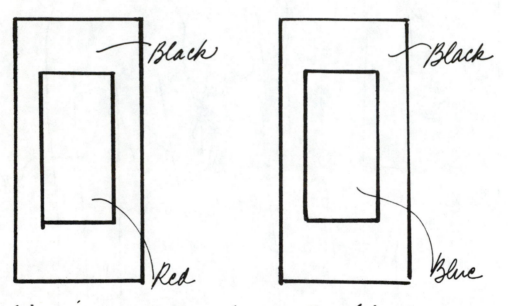

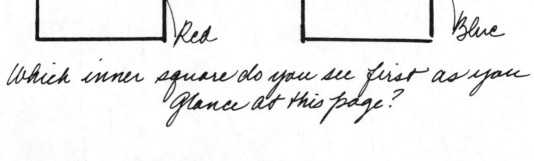

Which inner square do you see first as you glance at this page?

Red and
Black

Cobalt
and
Black

Cobalt
Blue

Red

Which color
focuses your
attention on the
face first?

Black

Black

Which coat
did you notice
first?

3. *Light values placed near dark colors make dark colors seem darker; dark values make light colors seem lighter.* This illusion of contrast is most important for judging the intensity of a color that is best suited for your complexion. A sunlight person with dark hair and a deep tan will make a light peach blouse seem pale. The paleness of the garment will, in turn, enhance her tan and make her skin tone seem darker than if she were wearing a light brown blouse. Dark velvet on a fair complexion will dominate it and make the skin seem even lighter. A pale complexion will have to balance the dark garment with more dramatic makeup or select a deep jewel tone rather than black to set off her delicate coloring.

Color the boxes as indicated. Evaluate the intensity of the inner shape. Contrast is one of the most powerful visual elements in apparel design. The designer tries to use enough value contrast to avoid monotony and create interest, but not so much as to overwhelm the viewer and create a confusing and overbearing garment.

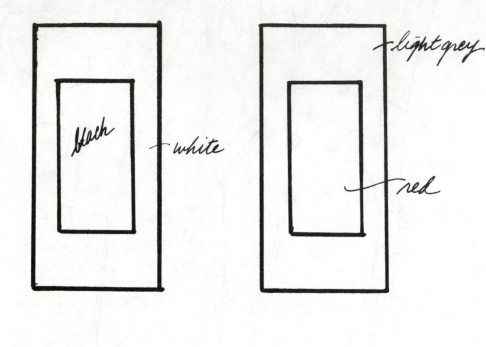

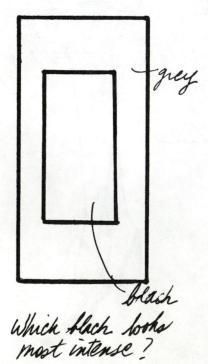

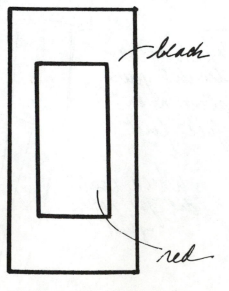

Which *black* looks most intense?

Which inner rectangle looks whitest?

Light
brown
hair

pale
makeup

pale hair

tan skin

Tan

Tan

Tan

Beige

Yellow

black

69

4. *Intensely colored clothing stands out against a duller background, making the wearer stand out. Neutral clothing against a neutral or more intense background makes the person less noticeable.* This illusion may be used in the design of uniforms, business clothing, and clothing for any individual who does not wish to stand out in a crowd. Dull, neutral, and dark shades make the wearer less visually apparent, and the person must make a verbal impact on his colleagues to be noticed.

Picture the classic waiter and remember how he often blends into the surroundings, camouflaged by his apparel.

Again, the boxes illustrate the truth of this principle. You can use this principle to advantage. Consider an occasion for which you are dressing. Is it a situation in which it is appropriate to try to focus attention on yourself? You can select clothing that is likely to make you stand out or recede into the background.

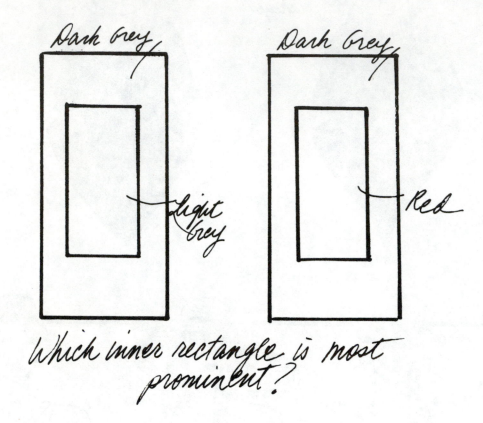

Dark Grey

Dark Grey

Light Grey

Red

Which inner rectangle is most prominent?

Dark Grey

Silver

Red

Which dress focuses attention on wearer first?

5. *Large areas of dull colors are needed to balance small areas of bright color.* This illusion is a logical result of illusion 2. Bright colors demand so much attention that they dominate large areas of dull color. Notice how coloring the blocks below proves this principle. Further, large, unbroken areas of bright color are often too intense to view for long periods of time because they create perception fatigue. The eye must have a resting space, a neutral area, so that the detail or accent color becomes interesting and important.

Apply this rule to dressing a person with low intensity makeup and complexion in bright clothing. The brightness of the garment will overwhelm the complexion and dominate the visual personality of the wearer. A high contrast complexion will be most beautiful in a bright garment with strong makeup color accents to balance the intensity of the garment.

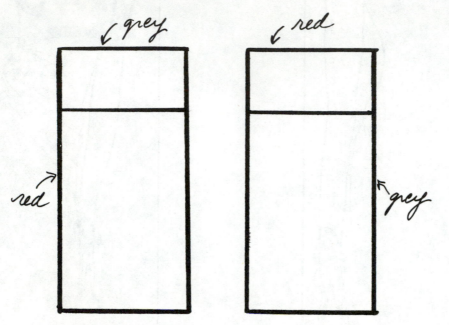

grey

red

red

grey

Which rectangle looks the slimmest?
Which rectangle focuses your attention at the top?

grey

red

red

red

black

black

6. *An uninterrupted flow of color lengthens and slims a shape. A horizontal division of color shortens and widens a shape.* Several different colors or values in an outfit tend to make the figure seem shorter and wider because the eye is unconsciously comparing the size and number of divisions and not moving as quickly as it would through a single-color composition.

The three rectangles demonstrate this illusion. Apply the principle to the garments on the right. The interrupted flow of values and colors make a person seem shorter than she would if she were wearing one, solid color.

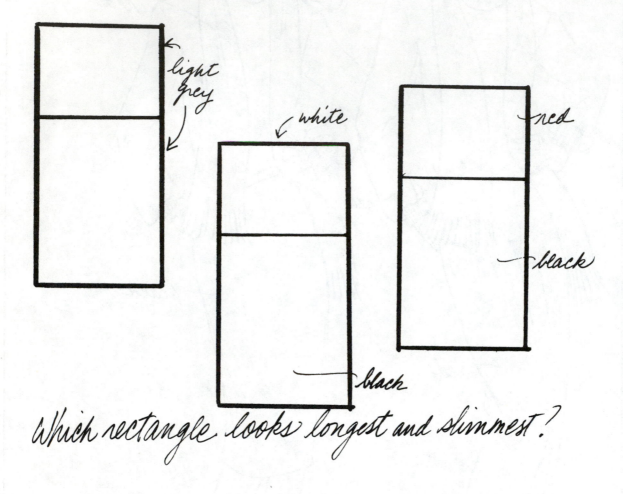

light grey

white

red

black

black

Which rectangle looks longest and slimmest?

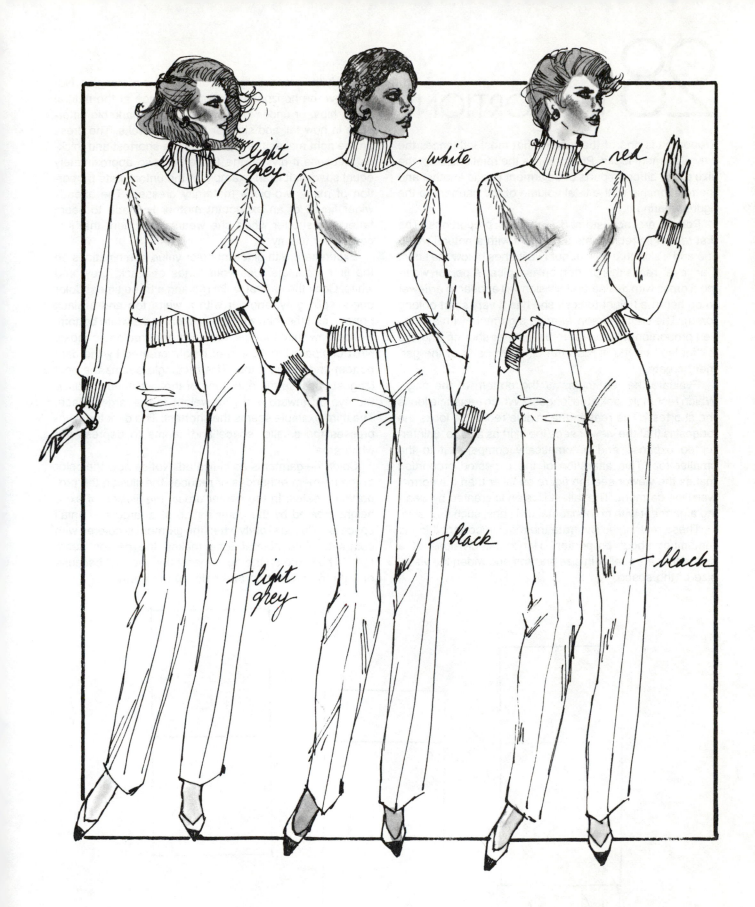

light grey

white

red

light grey

black

black

28 PROPORTION

Proportion is one of the factors that most influences the way a garment looks. Proportion is the relationship of the size of the different parts of a garment to one another and the relationship of the total volume of the garment to the figure wearing it.

People are accustomed to human proportions. The first rectangle represents a garment with a natural waistline and a skirt that falls about two inches below the knee. Our "eye" reads this proportion as typical. A person wearing a dress with this natural division will appear to a viewer to be her true height (unless she has a very short or long torso). The same person wearing a garment with a modified proportion will appear to be taller or shorter. The eye is "fooled" by the illusion the different parts of the garment create.

Evaluate the rectangles at the bottom of the page. Which rectangle looks the longest? Which rectangle looks the shortest? The reason the middle rectangle looks the longest is that the viewer sees the skirt as a large, uninterrupted expanse and automatically compares it to the smaller top. This alteration of the expected proportion makes the viewer see the figure as taller than the normal waistline garment. The tallest illusion is created by wearing a garment with no horizontal divisions, such as a shift.

These rectangles illustrate the most important thing to remember about proportion: Horizontal divisions of a space that are similar in size shorten and widen the visual size of the space.

Study the dresses that accompany the rectangles. Notice how the horizontal divisions of space at the natural waist, hips, or under the bust make a remarkable difference in how tall and slender the figure looks. The dress on the right makes the figure look the shortest and thickest because it divides the figure into two approximately equal spaces. It is an example of the unfortunate proportion of many two-piece maternity dresses. The already wider figure of an expectant mother is made to seem fatter and shorter when she wears a garment that just covers her tummy.

Experiment with different color value combinations on the first rectangle. Use your tones of black, grey, and white. Copy the natural waist rectangle three times. Color one a solid grey, another with a white top and a black bottom, and the third with a black top and a white bottom. Notice how much longer the solid grey rectangle looks. Next compare the illusion of height created by the dark bottom and the light top. This rectangle seems the next longest because the dark tone of the skirt tends to draw the eye downward and give weight to the larger space. The third example seems the shortest. The dark top compresses the smaller space and seems to depress the white area.

Color the garments as indicated. Notice how the color of the garment enhances or reduces the illusion the proportion creates. In the center dress, the illusion of extra height created by the combination of a large and small space is reduced slightly when the garment is colored with contrasts. One neutral tone makes the person seem taller. The figure on the right seems the shortest because of both the proportion and color of the garment.

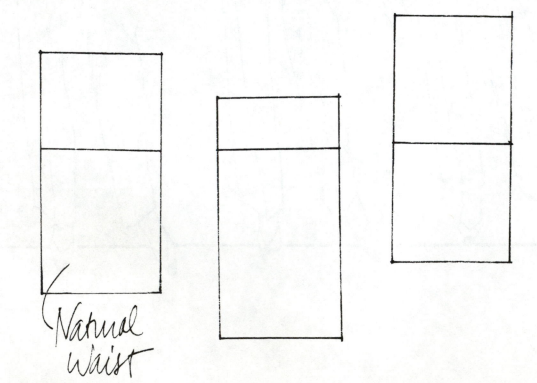

Natural waist

Purple

Off-White

Purple

Brown

Black

Hot Pink or Red

Beige

29 PROPORTION ILLUSIONS

The high fashion designer modifies proportion each season, creating garments that emphasize and exaggerate a part of the body to create a specific fashion illusion. Usually, designers use proportion to make women seem taller and thinner. This is the current ideal of beauty. The rules that create this illusion can be reversed to shorten the very tall person. A theatrical costume designer may play with proportion to make a character in a movie or play seem dumpy or fatter than the person really is. The rules of proportion are not good or bad; they are devices to emphasize parts of the body to create a specific look. They can be applied to problem figures to create an illusion that makes the person seem more like the fashion idea.

The dresses we just looked at are very simple examples of the effect of horizontal divisions. There are many possible variations on this idea relating to basic silhouette, parts of outfits, color counterbalances, and so forth. For example, reversing the large and small spaces in a garment will also create an illusion of height. The drop torso is an excellent way to lengthen the upper torso of a short-waisted person, an illusion which may balance the possible tendency of a lowered waist to reduce overall height. The drop torso dress will draw attention to the hips, which are often larger than the tops, so only a person with a slim hip can wear this silhouette, but layering will allow the less-than-perfect figure to wear a long torso garment. A vest, overtop, or jacket that covers the hip line past any bulges can be worn with a slim pant or skirt. The layered garment will balance the wider bottom and narrow top of a pear-shaped figure while making it seem taller.

A miniskirt will also make a person seem taller. This silhouette, especially the simple flared garment made popular in the 1960s by André Corregges, has a very youthful look. Slender, well-shaped legs are essential to its success. The relatively short expanse of the dress contrasted to the length of the leg makes the wearer seem taller. Dark hose and shoes emphasize the effect. Skin tone shoes and stockings will add to the height of any silhouette. A contrasting shoe pulls the viewer's attention downward and detracts from the impact of the garment's proportion. Feet look larger in a contrasting shoe.

Color tone and intensity emphasize and dramatize these elements of proportion. Dark, rich colors on the bottom tend to anchor the garments to the floor. A white or light top quickly leads the eye to the shoulders, neck, and face. Garments with no color contrast create a subtle illusion of height; a soft, neutral, or dark color has a greater elongating effect than a bright color.

Make copies of the low torso and miniskirt rectangles and experiment with color value relationships as you did in the first example. Compare the illusion created when the legs and shoes contrast or blend with the miniskirt example. Trace the garment examples and try other combinations of light and dark. Experiment to see how color values work in combination with the proportion of the garment. Evaluate how effectively these combinations create the illusion of height.

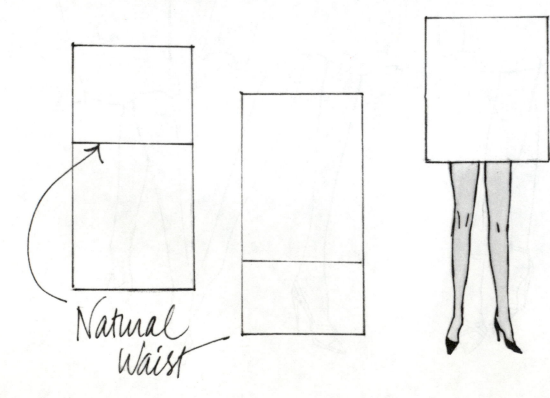

Natural Waist

Cream & Black

Black

Cream

Black

Cream & Black Dots

Black & Cream Dots

Black

Cream

Black Hose & Shoes

Black

Beige

79

30 PANT PROPORTION

Fashion designers play with pants and use a wide variety of shapes and lengths to achieve particular effects. Length determines the proportion of most pants. The illusion of height is created when the pant is long enough to cover a shoe with a medium to high heel. The pant forms a long, unbroken line from the waist downward. Pant fit is very important. A tight pant that clings to hip-line bulges and shows tension lines emphasizes the width of the hip and detracts from the illusion of length. A straight or slightly flared leg line creates the longest leg line and is the most flattering. A crisply pressed front crease line adds a vertical line which increases the illusion of height.

The two main categories of pants are jeans and trousers. They are made from different fabrics and have a different type of fit, but the principles of proportion and the leg-lengthening line are the same in both. Jeans are made from a heavyweight denim that is sturdily stitched and riveted so it can pull tightly over the waist and stomach. Trousers are usually made from a fabric like gabardine, flannel, poplin, or sheeting. The trouser cannot be as tight as jeans because the structure is not reinforced and the fabrics are often not as strong as denim or do not have denim's natural elasticity (called *recovery*). The trouser fits smoothly, but with some ease, over the hips and stomach and falls from the fullest part of the hip to the floor in a smooth line. Often women wear men's jeans. These fit low on the hip, making a good line for a woman who does not have a small waist and who has a straight torso.

Length is an important consideration for any woman wearing pants who is short and has a less-than-perfect figure. A pant that ends at the lower calf will make the wearer seem shorter, even if worn with matching hose and shoes. Fuller pants, like the bloomer and the jodhpur, will make the hips seem wider because of the contrast of hip fullness to the slim leg.

Shorts will also drastically affect the illusion of length. Short shorts worn by a person with long slim legs and heeled shoes will have much the same effect as a mini-skirt. Shorts add to the illusion of height because the leg length becomes the dominant area of the silhouette. A pant that ends at the top of the knee (the classic bermuda) can shorten the figure, especially when teamed with over-the-calf stockings and casual low-heeled shoes. Many horizontal divisions of the leg shorten the figure.

grey

Royal
Blue

Dark
grey

Royal
Blue

grey

Violet,
Aqua
and
Royal
Blue

Pink

Lavender

White

Chocolate

31 HORIZONTAL PROPORTIONS

A primary rule of proportion says that the viewer's eye automatically compares the larger portion of a space with the smaller space. The smaller area appears even smaller when surrounded by larger spaces. Which white square looks narrower? The effect of the silhouette of a garment depends on this automatic comparison of volumes. By exaggerating one horizontal line in the figure, the others can be minimized.

Visual perception of clothing also compares the volume of fabric to the actual size of the figure underneath. "Tricking" the eye to read size as having been created by fabric rather than by an excess of flesh is the primary goal of a designer. A woman can camouflage a figure problem by balancing the volume, color, and shape of her garment to create the illusion of a a slender body wearing a voluminous garment. The extremely thin woman can make use of the same balancing tricks. Designers often experiment with oversized garments because large clothes, properly fit and proportioned, can create the illusion of a frail, feminine figure.

Basic dress silhouettes emphasize different horizontal proportions. For example, the hourglass silhouette makes the waist seem smaller because the hip and bust or shoulder are emphasized. Volume might be added to the hips with a full skirt and to the upper torso with full, puffy sleeves. A small waist is often a beauty ideal.

The wedge-shaped silhouette contrasts a widened shoulder line with a narrow hip. The wedge shape tends to add height, especially if the shoulder extension is not too extreme and the skirt length falls below the knee.

The flared silhouette is a natural, comfortable shape that adds to height and makes the hip and waist seem slim. The legs also look slim, if the skirt is not too long. The flared skirt creates the illusion of a slim hip by contrasting the hip and leg size to the volume of the skirt.

Bad fit can overwhelm the intended illusion of a design. A garment that is skimpy or too tight does not elongate the figure. The horizontal wrinkle lines that are the inevitable result of too small a garment carry the eye across the figure, emphasizing width and not height or slimness. A garment that is too large may make the wearer seem bulkier.

Fashion often decrees the silhouette and volume of fabric popular during a fashion cycle. The public's eye gradually becomes accustomed to a new proportion, and it seems normal as it is interpreted from radical high fashion to wearable street fashion. The wise dresser follows the fashion trends, but interprets them as evolution, rather than revolution. Adopt the best silhouettes and details that flatter your figure. Drop fashions that are too radical or unflattering. Analyze your figure type and experiment with garments that draw attention to the best parts of your body.

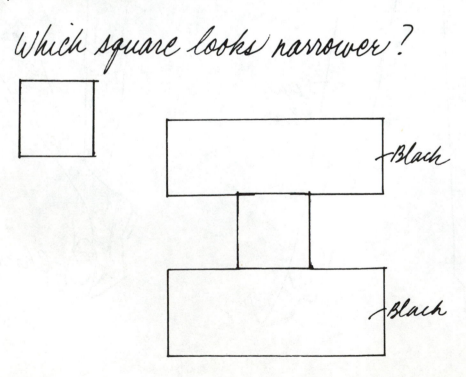

Which square looks narrower?

Black

Black

white

Red

Black

Light
Tan

Light
Pink

Dark
Tan

Black

Black

neutral

Grey

Skintone

Tan

Grey

83

32 LINE

Line refers to the edge or outline of a garment and the style lines that divide the space within a garment. Line creates visual effects because it leads the eye. Artfully used, line can create illusions to make the body look more like an ideal fashion figure.

Vertical lines emphasize height because they lead the eye up and down the garment. Less attention is focused on the width of the figure. Horizontal lines emphasize width, again because the line leads the eye. Diagonal style lines often have a slimming effect. Curved lines are feminine and passive. Curved style lines are used at necklines and in collars, ruffles, and other design details. The more exaggerated a curved line is, the more time it takes to view the contour and the more it focuses attention.

Study the optical illusion that is created by the linear diagrams on this page. The way the lines are arranged determines how long they seem, although all the verticals are the same length. The combination of a central vertical and two upward diagonals makes the vertical in the example on the left seem the longest. The third example from the left looks the shortest because the eye is distracted from the vertical with diagonal downward lines. The fourth example falls between the extremes. The vertical line is a focal point and the abrupt horizontals give the figure a strong, compact look.

These abstract examples illustrate the illusions that can be created by garments. The first example translates into the dress with the V neckline. The central vertical and two diagonals create a slimming and lengthening line. This illusion is enhanced if the V is emphasized by a contrasting blouse with a dark jacket and bottom or a contrasting tank top worn underneath an open blouse. The diagonal line in the second garment slims the figure more than horizontal style lines would, but it makes the figure seem shorter than the first example. The dress that has a strong horizontal neckline (called a *bateau* or *boat neckline*) makes the figure look the widest at the shoulder. Bateau necklines make narrow shoulders seem wider and balance a pear-shaped figure. A horizontal neckline also makes a long, thin face seem less so. The severity of the boat neckline can be softened with a contrasting necklace that falls in a graceful curve and adds femininity to the drama of the strong horizontal without diminishing the illusion of a wider shoulder.

Very tall women who wish to look shorter should use lines that break a strong vertical such as contrasting layers and accessories or mixtures of textures and colors.

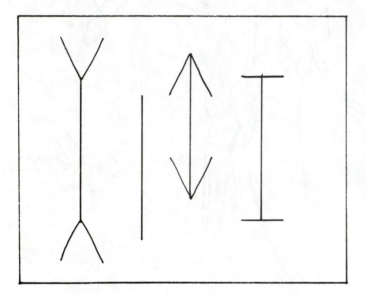

Tan

medium tan

Cream

Black

light Brown

Navy

All of the dresses have a strong vertical line and will slenderize and lengthen a figure. A single color or a subtle gradation of color with the dark tone at the hemline is particularly effective for lengthening a figure.

33 VERTICAL STYLE LINES

More than one vertical line in a garment divides the space of the garment, and the eye reads the combined spaces as smaller than the whole. To check this statement, look at the three rectangles at the bottom of the page and decide which looks the slimmest and tallest.

One type of vertical division in a garment is called a *gore*. Gores are separate pieces of shaped fabric that form a garment when they are sewn together. Gores form an unbroken line along the length of a garment and therefore they make the wearer seem slimmer and taller. Darts also form vertical divisions. They shape the fabric to the figure, but they do not connect the edges of the garment. Because they are not continuous, they "drop" the eye as it looks at the garment. The shorter, broken line makes a person seem shorter than she would appear if she were wearing a dress with a continuous vertical style line.

The garments on the facing page translate the illusions illustrated in the abstract rectangles to actual garments. Evaluate the garments before you color them to see the impact of style line only. Then color the garment as indicated. The first dress is called a *float, chemise,* or *shift.* This dress has a boxy fit with no waist definition. A tall, slender person wearing this style seems even taller. The float can also camouflage a thick waist and balance a heavy bust. Color the dress a light tone and evaluate it with the other two garments. Take a narrow marking pen and draw in a vertical stripe pattern. Notice how the addition of stripes emphasizes the vertical space and makes the dress seem longer and more slender than when plain. Narrow stripes are most effective; wider stripes often look very busy.

The single, center front seam is a long, slenderizing line. This effect can be exaggerated by color. A dramatic color difference between the two sides of the dress, half white and half black, for example, divides the space so the viewer sees two spaces smaller than the whole. Experiment with the optical illusions possible with two colors. On a tracing of the dress, color one side bright red and the other white. Notice how confusing this color combination is. Both red and white are advancing colors. The two used together visually enlarge the space instead of making it smaller. The secret of the slenderizing two-color trick is to make half the dress recede, while the other advances.

The final example is the *princess line,* also a slimming garment. The vertical lines are created by large gores from the armhole or shoulder. The figure seems taller and slimmer because the space is broken up into smaller vertical divisions. Now copy the dress on tracing paper and color the center panel black and the two sides white. How does the change alter the illusion of the garment? Too many vertical divisions will dilute the effect, and the garment will look confused because it lacks a clean styling theme. The busier a garment is, the more difficult it becomes for the average figure to wear. The tall, slender woman can wear a much more complicated garment than a person with a figure problem who will be overwhelmed with an elaborate dress.

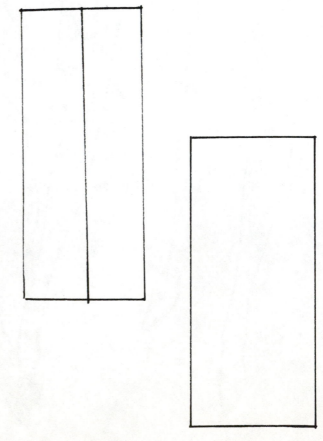

Black   Black

Black

Blue

white

white

Black

Experiment with the different illusions created by coloring the vertical segments different colors. Receding colors on the side of a garment focus the attention on the bright center strip. Imagine the similar illusion created by wearing a dark coat over a light dress.

34 HORIZONTAL STYLE LINES

Horizontal lines emphasize the width of the figure. Carefully used, they are very effective styling devices. Horizontal lines can attract the viewer's attention to a part of the body that should be emphasized to balance another part.

Narrow shoulders can be widened visually by a strong horizontal, such as a shoulder yoke. Soft gathers coming from a shoulder yoke add the feminine effect of curved lines and control the additional fabric needed over a bust.

A small waist seems even smaller if contrasted with a full blouse and skirt—the rule of contrasting proportion. The wider the belt, the more the area will be emphasized. A simple seam or narrow, self-colored belt attracts the least attention. No contrast at the waistline slims a thick waist. A horizontal division at the waist is a natural proportion.

Horizontal style lines are used in combination with vertical darts to fit a garment. For example, the waistline seam controls the ease needed to allow the garment to

fit the wider hips and upper torso. They can be decorative as well as structural, as in printed or textured fabrics.

Carefully used horizontal stripes correct some figure problems. A woman trying to balance large hips and a small torso can wear horizontally striped tops effectively. Border prints or details such as tucks at the hemline shorten a woman who is very tall because they pull the eye down and form strong horizontals to interrupt the vertical line of her height.

Drop torso garments visually widen the hip line and are most effectively worn by tall, slender women. Contrasting belts and style lines at the hip line minimize a large bust by making the hips seem wider.

Evaluate the rectangles at the bottom of the page. Notice how the vertical and horizontal lines work together to create many different illusions and how they translate into garments.

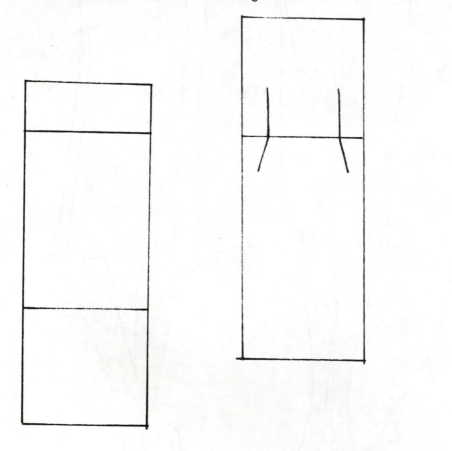

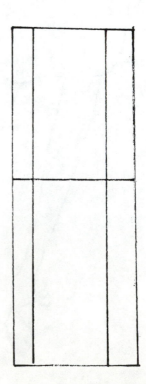

Red

White
Red

Dark
Grey

Dark
Grey

Coloring the first dress an advancing, aggressive color emphasizes the broad horizontal divisions, making it seem even wider and shortening the figure considerably. The style lines of the classic dart arrangement in the center figure emphasize the bust and hips. The wide belt in the outfit on the right visually expands the waist when colored in an advancing color. The verticals make this a slimming dress for a figure with a slender waist.

35 THE MOST IMPORTANT HORIZONTAL—THE HEMLINE

The most important horizontal style line in a skirted garment is the hem. The length of the skirt influences the entire proportion and all the other style elements of the garment. Hemlines are dictated by fashion. Public acceptance of a radical hemline change and new proportion takes time. The customer must get used to the new proportion and experiment with it. A skirt that does not conform to current fashion will look dated, but there is always a range of acceptable lengths. The trick is to determine the most flattering length for you within the currently acceptable fashion.

Experiment to determine which skirt length is most flattering *before* you go shopping. Your attention is often distracted in a clothing store. Many people concentrate on the color or the style or the price of the garment without evaluating its total proportion in relation to their own figure type—and that is the most important element in selecting a successful garment.

To experiment with skirt length, you must have a full-length mirror. Assemble the following materials.

1. A leotard or similar simple top.
2. A piece of dark fabric, wide enough to wrap around you and long enough to cover you from the waist to the floor.
3. A variety of stockings—skin tone, dark, and light.
4. A sampling of your shoe wardrobe including flats, medium heels, high heels, and boots.
5. A variety of belts—wide and narrow, dark and bright; also, a piece of half-inch elastic tied into a circle the size of your waist.

Wear the leotard. Wrap the fabric around your body like a skirt and secure it with the elastic. Start by wearing skin tone hose and flat shoes. Adjust the "skirt" to several lengths. Evaluate the effect created by the hem length in relation to your figure until you have found the most flattering length. Go through the same procedure with different stockings and shoes in different combinations. Experiment with the belts. Notice how a contrasting belt more clearly defines the length of the skirt and may require a

A flattering leg line is created when the hem stops below the fullest part of the leg's curve. This applies to above-the-knee lengths as well as below the knee. Dark hose will camouflage ugly knees when fashion demands shorter skirts.

slightly longer hemline to create the illusion of height. A general rule for slimming the leg is to end the hem at the fullest part of the leg. The skirt conceals the fullest curve of the leg and only a tapering column is visible.

Experimenting with skirt lengths at home before you go shopping allows you to adapt current fashion trends to a length that is flattering to your figure. You may have to repeat the hemline experiment to evaluate a new fashion length, but you can train your eye to see the best hem length.

The top of the boot should be completely covered by the skirt so there is no gap that detracts from the continuous line of the skirt. Dark stockings with a dark, low-heeled shoe balance a very short skirt. A medium heel adds to the illusion of height and is the most versatile. The short woman must balance her hemline and heel height with her total proportion. Too long a skirt visually shortens leg length.

36 DIAGONAL STYLE LINES

Diagonal style lines are very slimming because they direct the eye over the curves of the body at an angle and have a softening effect. Diagonal style lines can be used to create either symmetrical or asymmetrical designs. The human body is symmetrical, that is, it is about the same on both sides of a central line. The eye sees symmetry as the norm, so asymmetrical designs, in which the sides are different, have a more exotic look.

The angle and direction of diagonal lines are very important to the effectiveness of the garment. Look at the first rectangle. As we have seen before, the symmetrical V is very slimming, especially when a vertical line extends the shape to the hemline. The face is at the focal point of the V neckline. Shirt and dress collars form this shape when left unbuttoned. Jackets worn open and the collar of a tailored jacket create a V shape. A strong shoulder line is a successful way to style a garment with a V neck, because it balances the wider angle at the top of the neckline and creates a slight wedge silhouette.

Asymmetrical diagonal lines can be an effective and slimming way to style a garment. Notice how long and slender the middle rectangle looks. Color the corresponding garment as indicated. The black in the midriff area deemphasizes a bulky waist. Notice how the floor length gown adds tremendously to the illusion of height.

The final example uses the arrowhead division of space. Coloring it in tones of grey or subtly contrasting colors with the darker tone below adds to the illusion of height. The lightening of tone at the top leads the eye to the face, reinforcing the direction of the style lines and focusing on a good feature.

Asymmetrical diagonal lines can correct an unbalanced figure. A high hip or shoulder can be effectively camouflaged by using a diagonal to direct the eye away from the unbalanced part of the body. A low shoulder can be camouflaged by leaving it bare and covering the high shoulder with a diagonal neckline and slender sleeve.

On a balanced figure the diagonal in an asymmetrical design should run from the right to the left. The Western eye tends to follow a design in that format because of the habit of reading from the left to the right.

Some traditional sleeve treatments use diagonal lines in their structure. The raglan in the third example is the usual kind. The angle of the line is determined by the designer. Part of the bodice is incorporated in the sleeve. This line is very effective for slimming wide shoulders because it gives a soft, casual look to a shoulder line. Many sports jackets, inspired by men's wear, use this style line. Raglan sleeves slim the figure because they direct the eye upward and diagonally across the body.

Diagonal lines over the bust line call attention to and make the bust seem larger. The diagonal of a simple V neckline or a simple raglan will not emphasize the bust line.

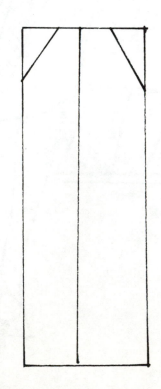

white

red

white

medium blue

Black

Navy

white

93

37 CURVED LINES

Curved lines are feminine. The gentle curve of a jewel neckline reflects the body's natural shape. A deep, curved neckline emphasizes the roundness of the bust and shoulders and has a sensuous, feminine look. The most exaggerated curved line in apparel design, the ruffle, has always been a symbol of femininity. The ruffle softens lines and imparts a romantic, fragile look.

Because the curved line holds the eye longer than a straight line, it focuses attention. The more exaggerated a curved line becomes, the more time it takes to look at the contour. The eye passes over the smooth areas of a dress and focuses on the ruffle. The face is highlighted by a ruffled neckline, the hands by a ruffled cuff.

The direction of a curve creates a specific illusion. A downward curve across the stomach makes it seem rounder. A blouse or sweater worn over pants or a skirt should be arranged with an upward curve over the stomach. This line is more slimming because it directs the eye upward and deemphasizes the roundness. A slight, even, downward curve in a fuller skirt flatters the legs. An upward curve at the front of a dress looks as if the bust or stomach is protruding and distorting the skirt. A jacket should have a slightly longer back length. The side seam will taper down from the front with a slight diagonal that is very slimming.

Curved style lines and the curved lines of ruffles, soft bows, and other details make the wearer seem more feminine and shorter. For example, a blouse with controlled ruffles worn with a tailored suit softens the appearance of the wearer without detracting from the businesslike image the suit imparts. A tall, angular woman can use these softening style devices very effectively. The shorter, more full-figured woman will emphasize her bulges if she overdoes the use of curved lines in an outfit. She can wear bows and ruffles, but they should be smaller and more controlled.

Curved silhouette lines camouflage the too slim and the too plump figure, if they are not overdone. The eye reads the soft curves of fabric bloused into a belt line as part of the garment and not as flesh. Notice how the garment on the right uses soft curved lines to camouflage bulges at the waist. Slight fullness does not distract from the vertical line and can therefore be slimming. Puffy, full,

curved lines emphasize roundness and make a full figure seem fat.

The same principles apply to hairstyles. A round hairstyle emphasizes the roundness of a face, while soft, vertical curves detract from the roundness. Reverse the rule if you are softening a long face or an angular jawline. The softness of a rounded hairstyle will make the long face seem more feminine and shorter.

Too Heavy eye make-up

A round hairstyle emphasizes the round face

Hot Pink dots on a grey ground

Hot Pink

Too many curved lines over-emphasize a full, round figure — The tight belt makes the figure short-waisted

An asymmetrical hairstyle with soft vertical curves slims

white

Navy

Same color belt in different texture — suede or leather

Navy

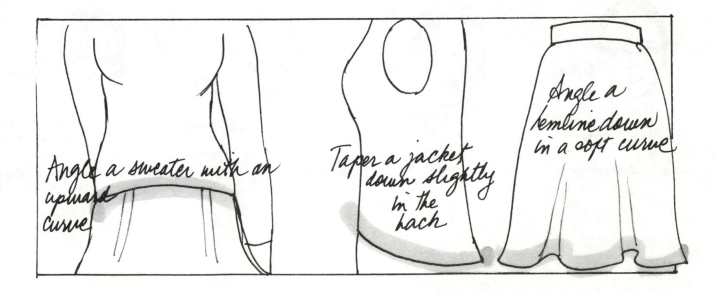

38 FACE, NECK, AND SHOULDER SHAPES

The personality and appearance of the face, neck, and shoulders can be greatly changed by illusions created by the lines of a neckline and hairstyle. There are four basic face shapes: oval (the ideal shape), square, round, and triangular. Let us review the effects of line and then apply them to face, neck, and shoulder shapes.

- Horizontal lines broaden and shorten.
- Vertical lines slim and elongate.
- Diagonal lines slim and elongate.
- Curved lines emphasize roundness and softness.

Look at your face, neck, and shoulders in a mirror. Match your face shape, shoulder shape, and neck length with one of the models in the drawing. The fashion ideal is a slim, oval face with a medium-to-long neck and a well-defined shoulder line.

The line of a hairstyle can modify face shape. Work with a talented hair stylist to find a style that is appropriate for you. Clip examples of hairstyles that you like and spend some time talking to the stylist before your hair is washed and cut. Try parting your hair in different places. Analyze the direction your hair grows and its fullness. Consider the effect of different styles on the shape of your face. If your face is too round, don't select a round, full style that will make it seem rounder. Choose an asymmetrical style with some soft vertical curves. A triangular face can be balanced by fullness at the chin line. Soft waves just above the shoulder will accomplish this. Fullness at the temples will diminish the impact of a square jaw. Oval shape faces can wear a great diversity of hairstyles successfully.

Next work with necklines to see how line can affect face and shoulder shape. Sit in front of a mirror. Use the same fabric you used in the skirt experiment. Drape the fabric around your shoulders to form the neckline shapes drawn on the next page. Experiment with necklaces of different lengths over the dark drape. Short necklaces make your face seem rounder and fuller at the chin line. They also tend to shorten the length of your neck. The deep curve of an opera-length necklace (24 to 28 inches) creates an illusion of height. Its almost vertical lines lengthen a round face and make the neck seem longer and more slender. The size of your bust will dictate the length of the necklace that is most flattering. The full-figured woman should avoid long necklaces that call attention to her full bosom. Notice how you can combine two effects, for example, broadening the shoulders with a bateau neckline and lengthening the neck and face with a V-shaped chain and pendant.

Make notes of the successful lines as you experiment. Try on several of your favorite blouses and compare them to the experiments you have made. Study this information so you have a specific idea which necklines are the most flattering before you go shopping.

The Ideal
The Oval
medium to long neck
Well-defined shoulders

Round
short neck
full, rounded shoulders

Square Jaw
Thick neck
uneven, sloping shoulders

Triangle
Too thin and long a neck
square, angular shoulders

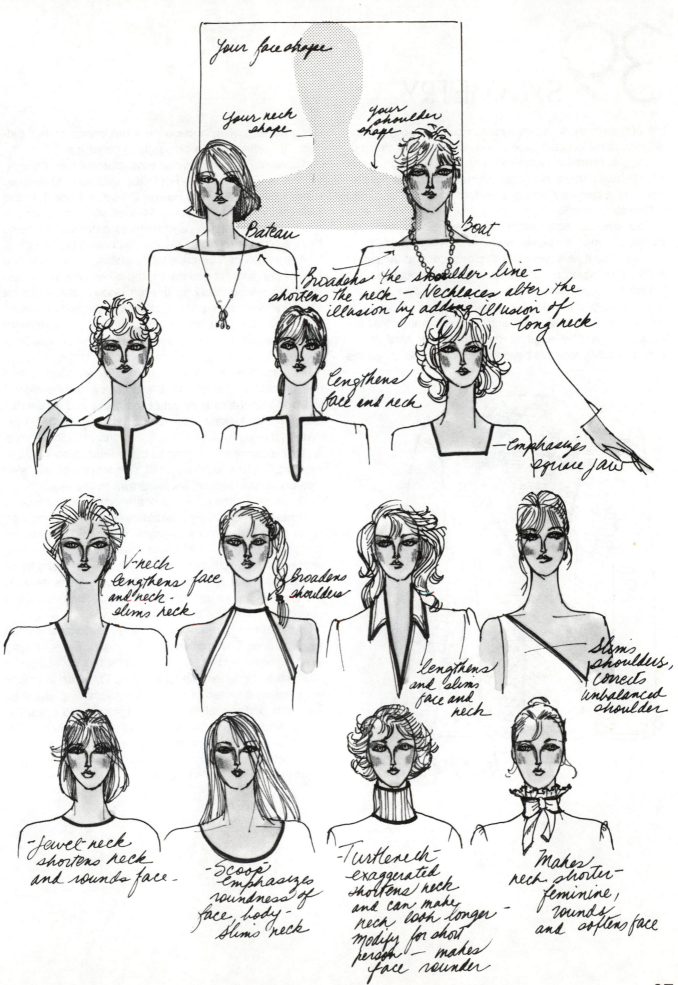

Your face shape

Your neck shape

Your shoulder shape

Bateau

Boat

Broadens the shoulder line — shortens the neck — Necklaces alter the illusion by adding illusion of long neck

Lengthens face and neck

Emphasizes square jaw

V-neck lengthens face and neck - slims neck

Broadens shoulders

lengthens and slims face and neck

Slims shoulders, corrects unbalanced shoulder

- Jewel-neck shortens neck and rounds face -

- Scoop emphasizes roundness of face, body - slims neck

- Turtleneck exaggerated shortens neck and can make neck look longer - modify for short person - makes face rounder

Makes neck shorter - feminine, rounds and softens face

39 SYMMETRY

The human body is visually symmetrical. The body is basically the same on each side of a central line (the median), creating a formal balance. A symmetrical design is the most logical and easily accepted arrangement for the elements of a garment and is therefore the most common design for apparel.

The eye corrects minor discrepancies in size and shape, so when an object is close to being symmetrical, the eye sees it as equal on both sides. Look at the jacket in the drawing on this page. Is it a symmetrical design? Actually, the jacket is asymmetrical. Your eye probably ignored the one asymmetrical detail. The eye follows the buttons up the center front and does not notice that the leading edge (the edge of the buttonhole side of the jacket) actually extends beyond the center line. Since the

Leading Edge

design lines, collar, and pockets emphasize formal balance, the effect of the design is symmetrical.

Garments of more obvious asymmetry require thoughtful design. They often do not follow traditional style lines. It must be obvious that design is planned and that the asymmetry is not a mistake. Balance and proportion are more experimental in asymmetrical garments because there are fewer formulas for the placement of style lines.

Asymmetry can be created by placing a detail on one side of the garment and not on the other. (We are accustomed to seeing detail on the left side.) A detail can be structural, such as a pocket, or a hand-painted or printed element in fabric design. An asymmetrical garment might have a placket or opening off the center line or style lines on one side of the garment and not the other.

Asymmetrical hemlines can create an alluring and unusual effect. The hemline should be carefully designed to blend with the total effect of the dress and be definite enough to look like it was done on purpose, not by mistake. In the garment on the left, the "handkerchief" style creates a hemline that echoes the asymmetrical detail of the skirt. It is best worn by a tall, slender person with slim legs because attention will be drawn to the legs.

Details focus the attention of the viewer on one side of a garment. Often a large, untrimmed space on one side of the garment balances an asymmetrical detail, as in the center garment. This two-piece dress was a tremendous success at many different prices for many sizes and types of figures. The soft drape of the bodice softens the bust line and gives a longer line to the torso. The overblouse effectively corrects a short-waisted figure.

Symmetrical garments may be accessorized to look asymmetrical. The garment on the right shows how an asymmetrically tied scarf, an off-center belt buckle, and a tilted hat add interest to a basic outfit. The scarf functions like a hairstyle parted to one side. By accenting one side, it creates a diagonal line that lengthens and slims the figure. Accessories such as a white lace handkerchief in a pocket or a boutonniere on a blazer create a slightly asymmetrical effect and add a surprise accent to a garment that gives it style and wit.

Mauve

Blue-Violet

Red-Violet

Magenta and Blue-Violet Dots

Lavender

Blue-Violet

99

40 SCALE

An effective garment must be in harmony and balance with the figure that wears it. The garment should not overwhelm or detract from its wearer. This is particularly important for the short woman.

Clothing made for commercial selling is usually fitted to a model 5 feet 6 or 7 inches tall. This means an average classical jacket length, depending on fashion, will be from 26 to 27 inches at the center back. A woman under 5 feet 4 inches will be overwhelmed by this garment. The length will make her look very short. The jacket usually cannot simply be shortened, because it is not only the length at the hemline but the cut of the whole jacket that is out of scale for the petite woman. She needs to choose garments that will add to her height and also garments that are cut for her smaller body.

A petite woman should carefully balance her skirt length also. A skirt that is too long will make her look as if she is wearing her older sister's clothing. If only the ankles and feet are visible, a short person will look even shorter. Enough leg must show to give length to the figure.

Accessories and details on clothing should be scaled down for a petite woman. Large pockets and lapels weigh a jacket down and make a petite woman look dumpy. Large purses and heavy briefcases give the small woman the look of a packhorse.

When a small woman is overweight, the problem is magnified. She may have to wear regular size clothes to accommodate her girth and then have problems finding the correct length. A jacket that covers the derriere might be too long to balance the figure. She will need to have larger style details to balance her figure without adding bulk to her frame. Small delicate details and frills will exaggerate her bulk.

The most effective way to dress the short, large woman is to select garments that emphasize the vertical line of the figure and that are simply tailored with a minimum of details. Subtle textures and patterns do not define the size and space of the figure. Subtle tweed suits contrasted with soft, lustrous fabrics for blouses and accessories that are a slightly lighter tone of the base goods fabrics are good choices. Bright, heavy accessories, including wide belts, shorten the figure.

Shoes are important to continue the illusion created by the right clothes. Shorter women are often tempted to add

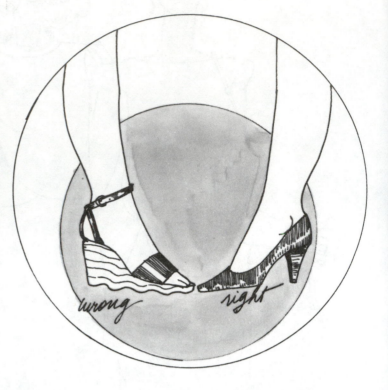

to their height by wearing platform shoes with high heels. These shoes make the feet seem out of balance with slender, short legs. Fuller, short legs seem bottom heavy and extremely clunky when wearing platform shoes. Medium-heeled classic pumps and casual shoes with few details slenderize the leg and make the wearer seem taller. Shoes that are a tone of the skirt or a neutral tone the same darkness as the stockings (beige, taupe, or grey) extend the leg line and make the wearer's legs seem slimmer and longer.

The garments on the facing page illustrate problems of scale. You can see how the length of the regular size jacket overwhelms the short woman. The size and amount of detail in the lower garment would make even a tall, slender woman seem shorter and wider. The hemlines and shoe styles are also wrong for the small figure. More suitable modifications of the outfits are shown on the right. A range of colors and different textures and fabrics provide enough interest to maintain the excitement and stylishness of the original designs.

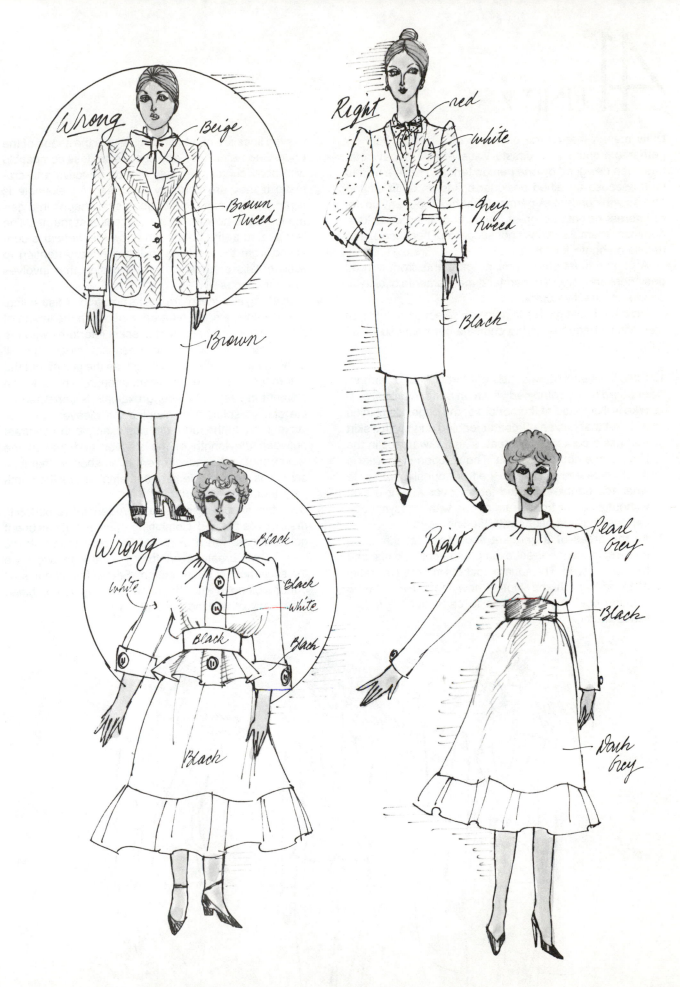

Wrong

Beige

Brown Tweed

Brown

Right

red

white

grey tweed

Black

Wrong

Black

white

Black

White

Black

Black

Black

Right

Pearl Grey

Black

Dark Grey

41 UNITY

Unity means that all the elements of a design work together to produce a successful visual effect. An outfit that has been designed by one person tends to have a unified look because a trained designer builds an outfit around one design concept. A garment that has too many points of interest or has too great a variety of lines or lacks a dominant theme is usually not successful because all the details compete for attention.

A person must often combine garments from several designers and should understand the elements of unity to create an effective outfit.

Here are some guides to help you select garments that have visual harmony and to combine garments successfully.

1. Style lines should be consistent throughout a garment or coordinates combined within an outfit. A typical mistake is illustrated at the bottom of the page. Combining a jacket that has an off-center leading edge with a skirt that has a center detail creates an awkward jog in the lines of the complete outfit. The solution is to wear a single-breasted jacket with the front-opening skirt or to wear the double-breasted jacket over a simple skirt without a center front seam or one with an asymmetrical opening that aligns with leading edge.

2. All the areas of a garment should reflect the same shapes. In the incorrect example the collar, cuffs, and hem are curved. The square pockets interrupt the unity of the design theme. Notice how the correct classic solution uses curved details to carry out the established theme.

3. Curved lines are most compatible with the shape of the body. Geometric lines and shapes are less compatible with body curves, but they can be effective and dramatic if they are carefully designed. An example is given of a dramatic use of geometric shapes in a garment. Notice how the angle of the line at the neckline is repeated at the bottom and how the vertical is continued from the neckline to the overlap. Attention to such details creates unity in a design that involves several shapes.

4. A small jog in a line interrupts its flow and is distracting. For example, a small difference between the length of a sleeve and the bottom of a jacket interferes with the horizontal movement. This does not mean that all sleeves must be the same length as the jacket, but the difference should be significant enough to be a design element in itself. The wrong example is corrected by the classic solution of aligning the sleeves with the jacket hem. In the more unusual example the contrast between the length of the sleeves and that of the jacket makes the jacket seem even shorter, that is, it serves as a design element that emphasizes the dominant theme of the outfit.

5. Style trim should be consistent. A decorative button is meant to be noticed. Combining a jacket that has bright gold buttons with a skirt that has contrasting plastic buttons will create a confusing outfit with two style trims clamoring for attention. Small, functional shirt buttons blend in with the fabric and may be combined with many other kinds of buttons.

Wrong   Solution   Same Jacket

Plain shirt

Wrong

classic solution

Dramatic use of geometric shapes

Wrong

classic solution

Sleeves and jacket same length

white

Black

Innovative use of length to achieve a special effect

42 FABRIC UNITY

The unity of a garment depends on the way fabric is used as well as on style lines. Here are a few pointers on the use of pattern.

1. Stripes and plaids that go in the same direction and are used on the straight grain should match, particularly on sleeves that hang parallel to the bodice. Stripes and plaids cut on the bias may be used with patterns cut on the straight grain, but the direction of all the bias pieces must match. The example on the left shows the distracting effect of stripes that do not match. Stripes should continue across the garment and tie in the torso and sleeves. Bolder stripes are more obvious when they do not match. Stripes or plaids that run in different directions can be used to create an effective garment and to avoid the problem of matching the pattern exactly. The example on the right shows a plaid used on the straight and on the bias. The bias plaid is very slimming.

2. If a pattern and a solid fabric are combined, the colors must be compatible. It is difficult to find an exact match between the ground color of a pattern and a solid. It is safer to combine a solid with an accent color used in the pattern because an accent color usually does not appear as a large solid area so an exact match is less important. However, the accent color must have enough weight in the print to make the relation to the solid color obvious.

   When matching colors, use the whole garment. The full impact of a print or a color cannot be seen on a small swatch. Compare colors in daylight. Store lighting distorts them. Do not just hold the fabrics together for an ''up-close'' look. You must look at the total effect of the match from a distance because that is how it will be seen on your body. Hang the garments up or have another person hold them about 10 feet away. Is the blend effective from a distance? Does the accent color in a print have enough weight to create a blend with the base goods? Is the ground color of the print compatible with the base goods?

3. If two or more patterns or textures are used in an outfit, they should be compatible in color and design. Colors can complement or contrast, but they must be related to one another. Patterns may be similar motifs in differ-

Black and White Patterns

ent colors or different motifs in the same color, but again the relation between the two should be clear. Pattern combinations are described again on page 146. The important point here is that you look for combinations that work together and with the lines of the outfit to create a unified effect. Repeat the test you used on prints and solids to validate the designer's choice.

4. Use the design principle of emphasis to create one focal point in accessorizing an outfit. For example, accent a garment at the neck with jewelry or wear an elaborate belt to create drama at the waistline, but not both. Wear very simple or no jewelry at the neckline with an elaborate belt, and wear an inconspicuous belt with an elaborate neckline.

Train your eye to analyze how a designer unifies elements to create a successful garment. When you see an awkward-looking garment, check to see which elements are in conflict with a design theme or if there is no design theme. This practice will make it easier for you to assemble parts of an outfit into an effective whole.

wrong

Bright Colors

Right

Right

43 RHYTHM

Rhythm is the repeated use of line or shapes to create a pattern. Orderly repeats of a line or motif direct the eye through a design with a flowing movement.

Uniform rhythm is the repetition of the same design element. This simple formula tends to become boring if there is no variation or accent added to the design. Color can make uniform rhythm more exciting by emphasizing similar shapes or certain parts of the garment.

The garment on the left illustrates uniform rhythm. A similar shape is repeated in the caftan many times. Study the illustration before you color it as suggested. The repetition of the wedge shape is pleasant, but the total effect is boring. With the application of color, the shapes take on new meaning. They seem to radiate from a central axis which directs the attention to the face. Color provides the drama the repeated shape lacks.

Progressive or graduated rhythm is the repetition of a shape in units of increasing size. This type of rhythm builds the interest of the viewer and draws the eye through the graduated units from the largest to the smallest. In the center garment the eye is drawn upward as the ruffles decrease from wide to narrow. This design does not have to depend on color for its effectiveness, but a dramatic color scheme will create an exciting garment. The size of the shapes is emphasized by the color changes, and the eye moves quickly through the interesting design of the garment.

Unequal rhythm is the use of unexpected space in a garment. It can have a dramatic effect when carefully used. The garment on the right shows a dramatic example of unequal rhythm in an evening gown. The color band would not emphasize a large bust or stomach because of the loose fit of the garment.

Equal rhythm is the most static and unimaginative use of repeated space. The uniform use of space contributes to a chunky, awkward design. Unequal or graduated rhythms are usually the most interesting ways to break up horizontal space.

Careful experimentation is necessary to design a garment that has a pleasing rhythm because the several spaces or design elements must be coordinated so as not to detract from the total garment. The difference of a few inches in the size of a space or detail is often sufficient to create an awkward design.

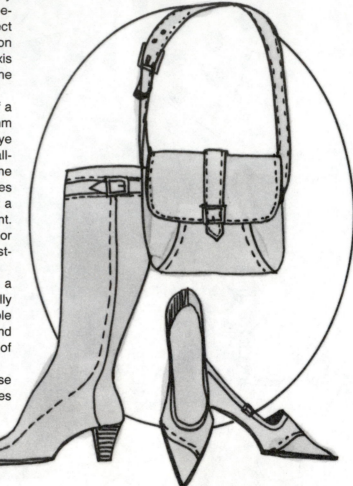

cream

cream

yellow

orange

cream

yellow

Yellow

Hot pink

White

hot pink

Black

Aqua

gold

Black

gold

orange

purple

44 EMPHASIS: COLOR CONTRAST

Emphasis is creating a focal point by outlining or exaggerating a detail so that it becomes the most prominent design element on an outfit. The most obvious way to emphasize a design detail is a sharp color contrast, but unusual shapes, different textures, a bold detail on a relatively simple space, and very bright colors also emphasize a design.

Several emphasized areas result in a disorganized and fragmented garment with too many focal points, but no emphasis results in a monotonous design. Interesting apparel must achieve a balance between order and detail. Too much organization creates a boring design. Too many focal points create a confused garment.

Emphasizing specific elements of a garment may strengthen the visual illusion it is designed to create. The suit shown on the left is an excellent example of emphasis by outlining the style lines. Contrasting braids or fabric bindings on the front edges of the jacket outline the vertical lines of the suit. The garment would not have as outstanding a vertical line if the jacket were trimmed in a matching binding. The loose but straight cut of the jacket adds to the vertical and can conceal a heavy bosom or thick waist. All these design elements contribute to the illusion of slimness and height. This formula was invented by the French couturier, Coco Chanel, during the 1920s. She did many versions of the braid-trimmed suit throughout her career.

The shoes at the bottom of the page were designed by Chanel to accompany her clothes. The black toe visually shortens the foot and makes it seem smaller. The heel and sling back have been revised according to the prevailing fashion of the period, but the basic formula of the light leather contrasted with a black patent leather toe has remained constant.

Chanel also designed a simple square handbag with a chain shoulder strap that can be converted to a clutch bag by tucking the chain strap inside the bag. The handbag is often quilted, which makes the leather very durable. Chanel valued classic, simple good looks.

Positive contrast is accenting style lines with a dark braid or trim. Negative contrast is accenting a dark suit with a white or light trim. Negative emphasis is effective for slimming a heavier figure.

The outfit on the right uses contrasting collar and cuffs to focus the attention of the viewer on the face and hands. Think of a policeman directing traffic wearing a dark suit and white gloves. He is dressed so his hands are the most visible part of his body. This format was also popularized by Chanel. The fresh white collar and cuffs have an ingenuous schoolgirl look. A small flower or crisp bow tie at the neck is another accent that directs the eye up the garment toward the face. When the garment is in a dark color, this is a very slimming and flattering illusion.

The color and material of the shoes and bag should be the same, or closely related, so the elements do not become too diverse and detract from the other details of the outfit. A neutral handbag echoed by the same color and detail in a shoe or boot will effectively pull together an outfit with several different textures and colors.

Cream

Navy

Cream
and
Navy

Cream

Navy

White

White

Navy

45 EMPHASIS: DESIGN MOTIFS

A bold or unusual shape will emphasize the area it covers. Hand-painted designs on full, loose caftans and coats are the signature of artist-designer Michael Vollbracht. These uninhibited garments are tremendously dramatic because of the use of bold colors and motifs to emphasize a certain area of the body.

There are several areas of the body that should not be emphasized for street wear. They are the bust, crotch, stomach, and derriere. Designers working with a large print often inadvertently place a motif on one of these areas. The wearer may feel uneasy about the garment but not understand why until she walks down the street and notices many stares automatically focusing on her bust or derriere. Shopping with a three-way mirror in an unhurried setting with honest salespeople is the way to avoid acquiring one of these garments with inappropriate emphasis.

Costume designers reverse the rules of streetwear design if they want to create sexy costumes to focus on the bust, crotch, and derriere. In the classic can-can outfit, the bust is accented with a contrasting color and outlined with braid. Many ethnic costumes also emphasize the bust line with a tight vest that is cut under the bosom and is worn with a contrasting blouse. Lingerie often emphasizes the bust with lace.

Designers that appliqué a motif on the stomach of a maternity dress are doing the expectant mother a disservice. Pregnant women should avoid wearing garments that focus on their rapidly expanding stomachs for street and business wear. Maternity wear should emphasize the vertical and use soft, flowing, one-piece garments.

Avoid placing a design or motif on any of these areas for street wear

OK for a funny T-shirt

Bavarian Beer Maid

46 SILHOUETTE

An apparel designer is a sculptor who uses the human body as an armature for soft fabric sculpture created to enhance the figure. The designer usually begins sketching the front of a garment in two dimensions and then visualizes or constructs the back and the sides to complete the three-dimensional shape. The size and shape of the garment are first perceived by its silhouette or outline. Then the eye of the viewer moves to the subdivisions created by the design elements to capture the total impression of the garment. These secondary elements—proportion, line, symmetry, scale, unity, rhythm, and emphasis—have just been discussed.

The silhouette is the dominant visual element of a garment and dictates most of its other design elements. The two main things that influence silhouette are fashion and the individual body. Fashion cycles often focus on a specific silhouette, but many kinds of apparel are used concurrently, and a person usually has a variety of silhouettes in her wardrobe at any one time. Fashion silhouettes are modified by adding fabric and padding to various parts of the body to create a specific shape. The silhouette usually conforms to the the shape of the body, but exaggeration is used to create a special effect or to emphasize a part of the body that is a current focus of fashion.

The silhouette that remains most constant is the natural silhouette or basic body shape of garments like stretch body suits, bathing suits, and leotards. There is little that fashion can do to modify the shape of a body wearing a leotard. The natural silhouette is best worn by an active, physically fit figure, but the comfort and functionality of body suits and leotards are desired by all figure types. Just because you do not have a perfect figure does not mean you should not wear a bathing suit or should go to an exercise class in baggy sweats.

The principles of illusion we have discussed can change the image of a body in a natural silhouette. The sketches on these pages illustrate some of the design elements that can be used. Cutting the leg line in an upward V gives the illusion of a longer leg. A leotard with sleeves minimizes heavy arms. Dark stockings and a bright body suit emphasize the slimmer torso characteristic of a pear-shaped body. Experiment with the amount of the upper leg that should be covered with a dark color. A deep shade for suit and stockings slims and lengthens. (Black is not a must. Try a deep burgundy, forest green, teal, or navy for a variety of body suits.)

In the garment on the left of the facing page, a bold diagonal stripe minimizes the size of the waist and bust. The color of the leotard should be determined by the size and shape of the legs. If your legs are slender and an

makes legs seem shorter

asset, wear a bright color. Heavy legs will look slimmer if you wear dark stockings.

The center figure shows how a short wrap skirt or slim gym shorts in a stretchy knit over a leotard can camouflage big hips. A contrasting design element at the bust balances the width of the hip. Legs look longer if short socks are worn with tennis shoes.

On the right a heavy bosom and a slender hip and leg line are balanced. Adding a vest or slim-fitted sweatshirt over the leotard would further camouflage this problem.

Red
and
Black

Dark
Tights for
heavy legs.
Bright for
slim.
(Black
or
Red)

Navy

Red

Navy

Navy

Navy

Burgundy

Red

Soft
Pink

47 NATURAL SILHOUETTE: CLASSIC BATHING SUITS

The one-piece bathing suit or maillot is a classic. This suit can be worn by figure types from matronly to youthful. The difference is in the under-construction of the suit and the cut of the outer shell. Fuller figures require a defined and supported bust which may be provided by a pre-formed bra cup in a durable interlining fabric. Junior suits for slim figures may have no undersupport or only a soft lining shaped with elastic under the bust. Most bathing suits are made from stretchable fabrics, either an elastic knit or a rigid fabric that has been elasticized. The term *maillot* is used to refer to the one-piece style.

Color is important to emphasize body areas and to frame the skin. Bathing suit colors should enhance skin tone. Dark, rich colors and bright colors enhance a tan. White is an excellent contrast to a tanned skin, but it is difficult to make opaque when wet, so it must be used with care in the area of the crotch and bust in a bathing suit. Pastels make the skin look washed out and are not often selected for bathing suits.

Function is important in the bathing suit. The wearer should be able to swim in it, and the materials should be able to stand up to the elements to which the suit is exposed. Manufacturers test a new fabric in sunlight, salt-water, and the chemicals most often found in a swimming pool. Elastic, trims, and underlinings are also tested to make sure they will last as long as the shell fabric.

Variations in the cut, color, or decorative detail of a suit may subtly alter the appearance of the body. Suits for heavier figures are often designed with a small skirt to hide the fullness of the hips and upper thighs. Slim legs can be made to look longer if the leg line on the suit is cut up slightly. A straight line at the crotch will make the thighs seem wider. The "boy" leg is a very short leg that stands away from the thigh and minimizes its bulk.

The suits on this page use diagonals to slim the body visually. The one on the left slims and highlights a small waist and minimizes the bust and hips, a good choice for the hourglass figure. The other suit slims the waist and hips and emphasizes the bust, perfect for the pear-shaped figure.

In the examples on the facing page, notice how bright pattern and decorative detail emphasize the bust. The blouson top camouflages a bulky waist. A skirt minimizes a protruding stomach, boxy hips, or heavy thighs. On a figure with a heavy bust, a skirt or boy leg balances the smaller hip. Verticals narrow and slim the figure from the bust to the hips.

De-emphasizes Bust and Hips

Black
white Piping
Red
Black
White
Red
Black

Slims and accents a small waist
Black

Camouflages full hips

Bright pinks & blues

Makes Bust larger

Marigold

minimizes waist bulge

Aqua

Camouflages a large waist

Makes Hips seam slimmer

Emphasizes Bust

Gold Metal Studs

Lavender & white stripes

Lavender

Slims waist, Bust and hips

Slims hips

Black

48 NATURAL SILHOUETTE: NOVELTY BATHING SUITS

Novelty bathing suits depart from the classic maillot into a variety of innovative styles. Generally, the less suit, the more perfect the figure must be to wear it effectively. The tricks of emphasis work with two-piece suits as well as with one-piece suits, but the exposed body becomes a more dominant part of the design as it becomes more visible.

The first suit at the bottom of the page would make a short person with a good figure seem taller. The strong verticals would also slim her figure. The diagonal lines of the suit on the right slim the waist and make the bust seem fuller. The contrasting pattern at the bust line enhances this illusion, and the dark bottom slims and deemphasizes the hips.

The top bikini on the opposite page would be best worn by a very slim and well-proportioned figure. A dark binding surrounding the bright fabric would make the bust seem larger. The strong horizontal of the bottom makes the hips seem wider, but the vertical of the exposed body makes the legs seem longer.

The modest two-piece suit beside it would highlight a slim, trim waist. A dark or bright solid or print fabric would emphasize the bust and hip line. The boy leg makes the upper thigh seem less full.

The gathered bra on the bottom example would fit and yet somewhat camouflage a very full bust but also would look good on a modest bust. A good fit and a dark color would enhance the effect. This suit would call attention to the stomach. The legs would seem longer because of the graceful, high-rise line.

The asymmetrical suit would slim the waist and emphasize the hip. The bust would be deemphasized by the diagonal lines and the more generous coverage of the top of the suit. The one-shoulder style and the larger coverage permit a more structured top, a desirable element for the full-busted or mature figure and for women who have had a mastectomy.

Broadens hips

slims waist

emphasizes bust

Yellow
lengthens legs

Bright
Tropical
Print

emphasizes hips - not upper thigh

emphasizes bust

lengthens leg

Blue
Violet
and
Aqua
Stripe

highlights stomach

minimizes bust

Black

emphasizes hip width

49 SLIM-LINE SILHOUETTE: PANTS

The slim-line silhouette hugs the body. It is the classic tailored silhouette. The slim-line pant silhouette is not effective for the very full figure because the garments follow the body too closely. Soft dressing silhouettes are more effective for a larger woman. Pants must fit well to enhance the figure. There are two main types of tailored pants, the snug jean and the looser straight-leg trouser.

Jeans are a practical garment because of their durability and comfort. They are now available in almost every size and are even modified for maternity wear. Jeans are effective on many figure types, but careful attention to fit is important for all women and especially those with heavy thighs or derriere.

Jeans are usually made in sturdy, heavyweight cotton twill fabric, such as 11½- or 14-ounce denim. They should fit snugly. The heavy fabric, reinforced seams, and sturdy zipper are designed to have direct contact with the figure from the thighs up. Denim tends to shrink when washed and then relax slightly when worn so it conforms to the figure. Jeans are too tight if they are uncomfortable at the crotch area, wrinkle through the thighs, gape at the zipper, or are uncomfortable to sit in. Jeans that force flesh up above the waist band are too tight.

Many confirmed jeans wearers wash their good jeans to shrink them and then have them pressed or drycleaned again so they become crisp and have a defined front crease. A smoothly fitted pair of jeans will make a person look taller because of the dark color, slim fit, and vertical front creases. Worn with boots or medium-heeled shoes, the leg will seem long and slim.

The trouser is often styled with darts or release pleats to compensate for the drop (the difference in measurement between the waist and the hips). Usually, the drop is 10 inches for a balanced figure. Trousers should fit smoothly over the top of the hips and fall in a straight sweep of fabric from the fullest part of the upper hip to the hem. Wools, lightweight cotton blends, and many other types of fabric may be used for trousers because the looser fit does not stress the fabric the way the snug fit of jeans does.

Pants that cling to the thighs or fit too snugly through the seat will emphasize the width of the hips and accentuate the fullest part of the figure. The front pleats and the pockets should not pull or gape. The crotch should not grab. The crotch line of a pair of well-fitted trousers should fall between one and two inches from the body. Look in a three-way mirror to check the fit of a pant over the seat to make sure there are no tension lines or underwear lines. Pants are too tight if any lines are visible. Many women elect to wear only panty hose under pants so there are no panty lines.

If your figure problem is a short distance between the waist and the crotch, beware of the pleated or tucked trouser and trousers with prominent pockets. These style lines add to the horizontal at the hip line, shortening the distance even further. Avoid the front zipper pant if you have a prominent stomach. Substitute side or back zip pants to play down this area.

The illusion of height is easily created with pants and a slim, fitted blouse. Pants automatically make a person look taller because the body from the waist down is covered with a single expanse of fabric. A slightly flared pant leg will also increase the illusion of height.

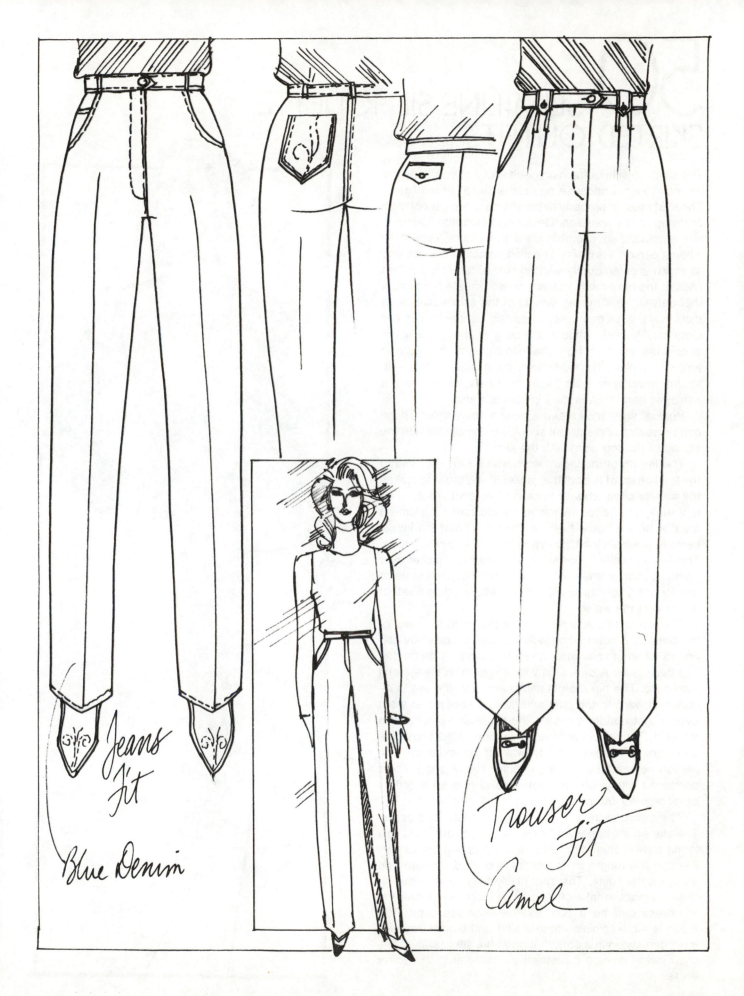

Jeans
Fit

Blue Denim

Trouser
Fit

Camel

119

50 SLIM-LINE SILHOUETTE: SKIRTED OUTFITS

The slim-line silhouette in an outfit with a skirt is flattering for most figures because no bulk is added to the figure. The skirt must fit properly to be effective. It must not grab or droop at the waistline. Designers often add elastic to the waistband to accommodate the natural expansion when a person sits down. The skirt should fit the hips and stomach area smoothly with no hint of tension. Tension lines at the hip or across the stomach create horizontals that defeat the slimming effects of the skirt's silhouette; they make a woman seem heavier, "stuffed" into her clothing. The skirt should not cling at the derriere but should fall smoothly from the fullest part of the figure to an even hemline. The skirt should hang straight at the side seams when seen from the front. A pegged skirt, with a narrower hem, makes the hips seem wider.

Vertical style lines make a person seem taller. These can be seams or pleats but should be compatible with the styling of the top worn with the skirt.

The length of the jacket worn with a skirt is crucial to the total effect of the outfit. A jacket that is too long makes the wearer seem shorter because the length of the skirt is visually shortened. A jacket should cover the crotch area or hit the figure high on the hip so that the jacket hemline does not lead the eye to the wrinkled crotch area. This is especially important when wearing a jacket over pants. A short woman will find a jacket that ends three or four inches below the waist is more flattering than one that aligns with the waist.

The length of the jacket also depends on the color of the bottom. A contrasting jacket should be carefully balanced for length because the body will clearly be divided into two areas. A dark skirt with a light jacket lengthens the figure. The hip area is minimized, and the eye is directed upward to the bust and face. A dark jacket worn over a light bottom shortens the figure and emphasizes the skirt. The less conspicuous division of the body by a one-color suit allows more leeway for jacket length. The person seems tallest in a one-color suit. A short jacket combined with a slim but softened skirt is an excellent proportion for the petite woman.

The tailored silhouette is also appropriate for dresses. The classic shirtdress has a slim-line silhouette. This flattering style is characterized by a front placket that carries the eye the length of the dress and tends to slim and elongate the figure. The front placket also makes this an easy garment to take off and on. A jacket worn over the shirtdress can be a conservative business outfit. The dress is more feminine than a skirt and blouse because it is often styled in a softer fabric with a silky texture. The crisp jacket gives a businesslike character to the softer dress.

Beige, Red
and Black
Print

Avoid the
equal proportion
of jacket and
shirt for a
taller and
slimmer
figure.

Red

Beige

Black

Tailored
Suit

Verticals increase the
illusion of height and
slim the figure when
made in a slim fabric

Dress-maker
suit
jacket
over a
shirtdress

51 | SOFT SILHOUETTE: PANTS

The soft silhouette has more ease and a fuller fit than the slim-line silhouette. Just enough fabric is added to the silhouette so that the clothing does not hug the body tightly. This is an effective silhouette for the heavier figure. The added fabric conceals the heavier torso, but there is not so much more fabric that the figure is visually enlarged.

Thinner fabrics are usually used for this silhouette. It is particularly comfortable in warm weather because the looser fit and thinner fabrics allow air to circulate near the body. This kind of styling tends to look dressier than tailored garments. Fabrics that drape, such as knits and soft crepes, are typically used for soft dressing. Lightweight, smooth fabrics like cotton sheeting are used in pants with a soft fit. Details typical of tailored garments, such as structured collars and pocket flaps, are usually inappropriate because the fabric is too light.

Shirring, tucking, and other decorative means of controlling ease are the styling devices used to create soft garments. They softly mass the fabric over the fullest part of the body avoiding the revealing precision fit and attention focus of seams or darts. Fabric can be carefully allocated to compensate for figure problems. A short-waisted person, for example, can make the torso seem longer with a soft top that is bloused over a wide belt, so only a portion of the belt is visible. The sketches on the next page show how effective this can be. The drape of the blouse over the belt visually extends the length of the waist.

Pleats and gathers are used to control the drop in soft pants. Fullness in the hip area will visually enlarge the lower torso. This style pant is appropriately worn by a figure with a small hip and a very full bust, as the example on the left shows. The hip line is not overexaggerated, but a subtle balance of width equalizes the bust. The drop torso makes the waist look longer, often a problem with a full-busted figure.

The pear-shaped figure will have to use more caution when wearing the soft pant silhouette. A short woman will have particular difficulty with this silhouette, because the soft top will turn her into a rectangular shape if it is not balanced with a smooth, sleek bottom.

A slender, well-balanced figure can wear this silhouette well. A soft pant outfit, like the one on the right, will be especially flattering in one color on a slender figure of any height. The detail at the hip line is balanced with a slightly fuller sleeve and a soft bow at the neck.

The mobility allowed by this style makes it appropriate for exercise garments. Pants with a drawstring or elastic waist and rib knit or elastic cuffs let a person run or exercise without the interference of flapping legs.

Soft Marigold

Periwinkle

Red-Violet

52 SOFT SILHOUETTE: SKIRTED OUTFITS

Soft dressing in skirt silhouettes includes dirndls, gathered skirts, and flared skirts. This is one of the most flattering silhouettes for the fuller figure. The skirt avoids many problems of the soft pant silhouette because the visible part of the leg slims the silhouette. Soft dresses and skirts are most often made in lightweight fabrics and the fullness is attributed to the added fabric instead of flesh. Bows, ruffles, tucking, and pleating details are typical of this feminine way of dressing. The moderate skirt silhouette is basically rectangular and adapts itself to concealing a full waist or hips. It is also effective in making a tall, angular woman look more feminine. Again, the trick is the addition of soft fabric and details to cover the angular bones and joints.

The garment on the left illustrates the classic float or shift. This type of garment flatters the heavier, shorter woman because the lack of definition of the waist gives a long line that accentuates a person's height. The important elements, when styling a dress to flatter the short, bulky figure, are pattern and color. Vertical stripes lengthen and slim the figure. Deep, rich, solid tones streamline a bulky torso. Dark colors with accents at the neck and wrist direct attention to the face and hands and diminish the visual importance of a heavy body.

The soft flared skirt is one of the most flattering garments for any figure type. The wedge shape is slim at the hips and then flares at the legs, which then look slimmer by contrast. A top with a soft blouson and an understated waistline will be a good line for many figure types.

Details within this formula can make it more effective for specific figure types. A woman with a large bust should wear blouses with a controlled amount of ease. Gathered fabrics tend to lead the eye to the source of the gathers, so concentrate the fullness at the neck or shoulders if you have a full bosom. The woman with a smaller bust can select a garment with more ease closer to the bust. The hourglass figure can make the most of a flared skirt and full blouse by dramatizing her small waistline with a bright belt. The soft areas of the blouse and flared skirt will minimize the width of the bust and hips and balance her assets. The pear-shaped figure should wear a fuller blouse and a smoother flared skirt to balance her figure.

The dirndl and gathered skirts often pose a problem because they increase the width of the hips and stomach. Too much ease at the waistline gives a square hip look. The dirndl skirt does not have a flared hemline, and so it looks boxy. This is an appropriate silhouette for a very slender person who wants to look larger below the waist.

The kind of fabric and the way the skirt is cut affect the amount of fullness the skirt can effectively have. A firm,

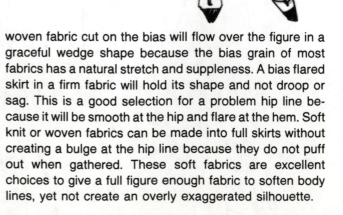

woven fabric cut on the bias will flow over the figure in a graceful wedge shape because the bias grain of most fabrics has a natural stretch and suppleness. A bias flared skirt in a firm fabric will hold its shape and not droop or sag. This is a good selection for a problem hip line because it will be smooth at the hip and flare at the hem. Soft knit or woven fabrics can be made into full skirts without creating a bulge at the hip line because they do not puff out when gathered. These soft fabrics are excellent choices to give a full figure enough fabric to soften body lines, yet not create an overly exaggerated silhouette.

Black
and
Beige

Cream

Cream
and
Red
Print

Beige, Black
and Red
Stripe

The dirndl skirt makes the hipline square when made in a stiff fabric.

125

53 WEDGE SILHOUETTE

The wedge silhouette increases the visual width of the body at the shoulder. Width at the shoulder makes the hips seem narrower. This illusion is heightened when the skirt or pants are slim fitting to contrast with the wider shoulders. The silhouette makes a person look taller.

The wedge is the classic men's suit silhouette. It represents the ideal male figure of wide shoulders and slim hips. Men's wear is tailored to conform to this ideal. Padding widens and squares the shoulders, lapels reinforce the diagonal, and padding and stiff interfacings add width to the chest.

The wedge silhouette for women has been popular when women are assertive in their social roles. It was extremely popular during World War II. Women worked outside the home and assumed more responsibility for the welfare of the family while men were away in the armed forces. The late 1970s and early 1980s saw a return of the shoulder wedge as a fashion silhouette. Women were again entering the job market and assuming a more masculine role in the society.

Shoulder pads do more than square the shoulder line and make a person look taller. The added construction supports the garment while it is being worn. The shape of the body has less influence on the shape of a tailored garment than on a soft one. Shoulder pads also support the garment while it is on the hanger. This enhances the hanger appeal of the garment and allows a consumer to picture what the garment will look like on a body before trying it on.

Extreme shoulder extension tends to overpower the small figure. Short women should not wear too large a shoulder pad or too puffy a sleeve. The wedge does enhance height, so it is appropriate for a petite person's wardrobe, but for the silhouette to be effective, the shoulder line must be modified to suit the height and weight of the wearer.

Garments can be styled to have a wedge silhouette by adding shoulder pads or details, full sleeves, or large collars. Shoulder pads are usually smaller for a soft garment than for a tailored one. Large, puffy sleeves in crisp fabric, like taffeta or silk organza, duplicate the wedge silhouette. Evening wear is often designed with such "leg-o-mutton" sleeves, and they can be quite effective on a long slim dress, as the illustration at the bottom of the page shows.

Bat-wing, dolman, and raglan sleeves cut with a great deal of fabric under the arm create a wedge silhouette. This line is good for a tall woman with a full bosom and a slender waist and hips. The full sleeves minimize the top of the body and focus on the slim hip area. A short-waisted person can carry this silhouette if it is an unbelted or overblouse style with a long torso that visually extends the waist.

The sketch on the left is a tailored garment with a moderate amount of shoulder emphasis. This classic look would be appropriate for business and could be adapted to more casual wear as well.

The soft dress in the center uses pads, epaulets, and sleeve ruffle to support the novelty shoulder line. The important element of this garment is the relative narrowness of shoulder line. The sleeve starts one inch in from the natural shoulder line. The puff does not look as broad, yet carries out the wedge silhouette in a soft dress style.

The blouse on the right has a dolman sleeve and a drop-torso detail that would be appropriate for a tall as well as a short woman. The overblouse would camouflage a short-waisted figure.

Cream

Forest
green
and
red

Forest
Green

Red

Forest
Green

Cream

54 HOURGLASS SILHOUETTE

The hourglass is a feminine silhouette because it emphasizes a full bust and wide hips. The narrow waist contrasts with the wider areas of the figure and visually "proves" the delicacy and smallness of the figure despite the fullness around it. The hourglass figure has been a dominant theme throughout fashion history.

In the past waist cinchers and corsets were used to pull in the waist. Sometimes these cruel efforts to make the flexible waist area smaller were so harsh that women fainted or suffered broken lower ribs from being corseted. This practice made women's waists consistently smaller. During the 1960s, there was a turn toward shift dresses and the small waistline was "lost" for about a decade. Clothing manufacturers found that women's natural waistlines had increased over an inch per size when belts returned to fashion. The decade of the seventies has seen a steady increase in the size of garments. Manufacturers cut their clothing larger to flatter women and to emulate the more expensive houses. Women expected to wear a size smaller than usual in a better garment, and gradually all manufacturers have enlarged their clothing to new typical sizes. The chain stores are particularly emphatic about setting fit standards for the hundreds of suppliers they have. These stores publish size specifications for their manufacturers and measure the garments they order to make sure they conform to their specifications. General merchandise in department stores and speciality stores will vary widely in fit.

The visual illusion of a small waistline is still possible through design techniques similar to those used in the past but without the severe corseting. A contrasting belt defines the waistline. Color the belt black in the sketch on the left. The waistline recedes and seems smaller. Color the center belt a bright red or pink. This advancing color will catch the eye and will focus attention on the smallness of a thin waist. However, the brightness would make a thick waist more noticeable, so a bright belt is a good selection only if you have a slim waist. Remember always to minimize the areas that you do not wish to call attention to with neutral, subtle shades. Highlight the positive with color.

The hourglass effect is enhanced by a longer-than-knee-length skirt. The sweep of a long, flared skirt makes the waist seem even smaller, and, of course, the person taller. A fitted waistline, a slightly full sleeve, and a very full skirt constitute an evening and wedding gown formula that has been successful for many years because of its femininity. The sketch on the right is a typical "romantic" dress featuring an hourglass figure. The mid-tone pastel of the belt against a cream garment focuses some atten-

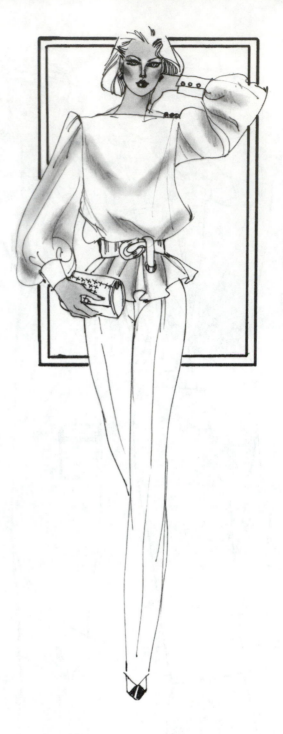

tion on the waist area, but it is subtler than the effect of a strong or dark color.

Petite women may wear the hourglass silhouette, but they should modify the proportion and volume of the skirt so they are not overwhelmed. A small woman with a full bosom will find this look unflattering. She will seem very short waisted and should not attract additional attention to her waist with a snug, contrasting belt. A woman with a bulky torso or a large waist should opt for another silhouette.

The hourglass silhouette can be attractive as a pant outfit. The soft pant and peplum top, accented with a wide belt, will create this illusion. This silhouette should be worn by a tall, well-proportioned person.

White

Red

White

White

Black

Red
and
black

White
ground

White

light
blue

White

129

55 FULL-VOLUME SILHOUETTE: SKIRTED OUTFITS

The full- or extreme-volume silhouette is sometimes a popular fashion. Extreme silhouettes occur in fashion at varying times. They sometimes occur as a reaction to the conservative "ladylike" fashions of a period. They are often done by experimental designers who want to make a dramatic statement to set themselves apart from the acceptable clothing forms promoted by commercial fashion. Designers often create dramatic "showpieces" to establish a new ideal of beauty or a new clothing concept, to shock people into trying something new, and to attract the attention of the press. These statements reflect trends in the society, and the garments must be modified to be sold and be modified greatly to be appropriate for the business world.

The figure is minimized in the full-volume silhouette, and the draping and design of the fabric become most important. A mix of prints and textures can be used as the figure becomes less visible and the decorative elements of fabric and design take over. Several layers may be worn to achieve the mix of fabrics and the full look. Lighter fabrics have movement and can be styled into several layers to create the illusion of fabric bulk and not body bulk.

Large figures have a variety of wardrobe choices when fashion decrees fullness is beautiful. A simple garment with graceful, flowing lines will be most effective for a very large figure. This woman tends to wear an extreme-volume silhouette out of necessity, even when slimmer fashions are in style. Light fabrics controlled with gathers and tucks will flow over the bulges and camouflage the bulk of the upper arm or thighs. Skirts are most flattering for the very large figure. Caftans are popular because they offer a long, continuous line that covers the figure without attempting to fit any area snugly. These garments are best worn for casual events at home. They are not appropriate for street or business wear. Color and accents can be used dramatically, but they should focus attention on an appropriate area of the body. Scarves at the neck and shoulders accent a pretty face. Jewelry can provide contrast in the outfit and direct attention to the face or hands. Tonal hose slim the legs and provide a good contrast for the width of the skirt.

The full-volume silhouette is a classic and acceptable theme for outerwear, even when the slim-line silhouette is fashionable for other clothes. Bulk conveys the impression of warmth as well as physically providing it. Furs, heavy wools, down or fiber-filled quilts, and heavy leathers are typical cold weather outer layers. Bulky sweater knits worn over wool shirts and long skirts are popular during the winter. Coats are voluminous enough to cover

suits and dresses. Capes and large shawls are popular additional accessories.

The petite woman will have to balance the size of her clothes and accessories to achieve the look of volume without being overwhelmed by her clothing. If you are small, wear a slightly shorter skirt. Keep the colors of all the components of an outfit in one tone. Choose smaller handbags and scarves. Wear boots or stockings and shoes to match the color of your skirt to appear taller. Select a medium-bulk fur with a slim style. Contrast a bulky outerwear wrap with slender skirts and tops.

Turquoise

Light Khaki

Turquoise

Cream

The Very Large figure should wear simple, clean volume silhouette garments in light colours.

Extreme volume silhouettes imply & provide warmth

Olive Drab

Red!

The Petite figure should have scaled-down volume in proportion to the figure.

56 FULL-VOLUME SILHOUETTE: PANTS

The extreme-volume silhouette is difficult for most figures to wear when fashion decrees pants should be cut very full. This silhouette emphasizes the width of the hips and legs and makes a person seem shorter, so only a tall, slender person can wear the full pant. The most successful way for others to wear the full silhouette is to modify it to keep the volume above the hip line and contrast it with a slim-line pant. Dark pants will make a person seem taller, even when she wears a bulky top. This modified silhouette is the typical cold weather active-wear outfit. A parka or bulky sweater is worn over slim-line pants for mobility when skiing or running.

The outfit on the left is an effective combination of a full jacket and a slim pant. The eye accepts the bulk for warmth and does not read it as exaggerated. The slim line of the pant establishes the existence of a small body. The longer jacket with only the slimmer lower leg showing is good camouflage for a full torso and upper leg.

Large figures sometimes wear bulky pants hoping the fabric volume will hide their figure problems. The total silhouette is usually too overpowering to be attractive. A large figure should modify the silhouette by wearing a straight-leg pant and a loose tunic or long vest that covers the thighs. One deep, rich color or a neutral tone will be the most slimming. Bright accents added at the face and hands are attractive. The additional layer will visually lengthen the torso and avoid focusing attention on the waist. The continuous line of the pants will make the large person seem taller, yet the derriere will be covered, usually a problem area for the large woman. The center example shows how effective this line is for the very large woman.

Full-volume summer clothing is often made from lightweight fabrics gathered at the waist or worn loose enough to allow air circulation near the body to keep it cool. The outline of the body is often visible through the sheer fabric, and even though the garments are full, the illusion of the body is slender. This is a very sensual look and is appropriate for many kinds of figures.

The diversity of silhouettes usually found in an individual's wardrobe reflects the many activities in which she participates and changes in the stylish silhouette. Most people do not regularly purchase an entirely new wardrobe, but use older components worn with newer garments to create fashionable and functional outfits. People with figure problems often dress in silhouettes based on a formula that is successful for them and ignore fashion changes.

Red

Light
Olive
Drab

Black

Brown,
Camel and
Rust

Peach

Dark
Peach

Red

Black

Camel

The large figure
can successfully
camouflage bulk
with slim soft
layers

Brown

Tall, slender
figures can
wear extreme
volume clothes
in warm
weather.
Lightweight
gauze
is semi-
transparent..
and very
alluring

Peach

57 FABRIC

A commercial designer selects fabrics the way you should select your wardrobe, using price, esthetics, season, fashion, and suitability for a specific purpose as criteria. Designers are trained to see a piece of fabric and imagine how it will look when sewn into the kind of garment they are designing. The successful home sewer must develop this talent also.

In purchasing clothes you have the advantage of being able to see how the fabric works for a particular garment. But, you should still consider the following things about the fabric before deciding to purchase a garment:

1. *Fiber.* Is the fiber suited to the season? Will it perform well and be easy to take care of? Are you allergic to it?
2. *Weight.* Is the garment the correct weight for your wearing requirements? Will it be appropriate for the season and climate in which you will be wearing it? Is it too specialized for the typical weather you will live in, that is, will it be wearable for only a very short season?
3. *Texture or hand.* Is the fabric the correct stiffness for the garment? Does it drape well? Does it have a pleasant feel?
4. *Surface interest.* Does the color, pattern, and texture of the fabric please you? Does it flatter you?

These four elements determine the character of the fabric. They also dictate many of the limits on styling. The designer who created your garment is familiar with all types of fabric. You, as a customer, can evaluate a garment's potential use and life by how the fabric has performed for you in the past.

Designers try to select fabrics that have current fashion appeal. Usually a new fabric trend begins in designer clothes and expensive ready-to-wear. Like the style, the fabric is adapted for the mass market and imitated in other fibers and constructions. Lightweight fabrics are in fashion when silhouettes are voluminous. Tailored, smooth fabrics are popular when construction details are important. Textured suitings and tweeds are in vogue when women's wear is fascinated with men's wear.

Specific fabrics are typical of apparel categories. Lustrous, metallic fabrics are dressy. Stretch knits are popular for active wear. Wools are typical for suits and expensive sports wear. Cottons are appropriate for many categories of apparel, from men's shirtings to children's wear.

A designer selects basic fabrics for the tailored tops and bottoms in the line. This should also be true of your wardrobe selection. Novelty fabrics work well in some tops, in soft garments like dresses, and in accent pieces. Note how the two basic pieces in the wardrobe at the right can be combined with many of the tops to create a variety of looks appropriate for day or evening. Imagine some other color combinations that would be appropriate for your palette and color in the pieces so they make a logical group of clothes appropriate for a weekend trip to a city.

Color is the first thing that attracts a customer. Your next instinct is to reach out and touch the fabric. Esthetics combined with practicality are the most important aspects of selecting the right fabrics for your wardrobe.

Classic Travel Wardrobe

tie

scarf

Base Goods
Pieces

sweater knit

Tonal and
contrasting
belts

casual shoe

classic pump

58 FIBERS

Fibers are spun into yarns that are woven or knitted to produce fabrics. The natural fibers are cotton, wool, silk, linen, and hair fibers like cashmere and camel's hair. Traditionally, these fibers have been considered appropriate for a specific season. Wool and the hair fibers are made into fall and cold-weather fabrics. The natural crimp in the fibers makes them easily woven or knitted into lofty fabrics which trap a layer of warm air close to the skin to protect the body against cold. Smooth, lightweight versions of wool-fiber fabrics are gabardine and challis. These can be worn in all but the hottest climates.

Silk is also versatile and can be worn year-round, though often as a blouse under a warmer garment during the fall and winter.

Linen and cotton are warm-weather fabrics because they are cool, absorbent, and easily washed. Cotton can also be woven as a sturdy base goods fabric, such as bulky corduroy, that can be worn for cooler temperatures.

Synthetic fibers have been developed to imitate natural fibers. They are woven to resemble natural fabrics. Synthetics may be blended with natural fibers to increase the resemblance to the feel and characteristics of a natural fabric. Rayon, polyester, and nylon are typical synthetics.

The choice of fiber is important when you consider how you will have to care for a fabric. Wash-and-wear or easy-care characteristics are generally built into polyester fabrics. Easy care is particularly important for garments that will be laundered frequently, like children's wear and work clothes and uniforms. Rayon, even though it is a cellulose fiber like cotton and linen, is usually not as durable as the natural fibers and will not stand up to constant washing.

Some fibers react badly to water and must be dry-cleaned. Wool and silk are usually dry-cleaned, although some fabrics can be hand washed and ironed if care is taken to use a mild detergent and the proper washing and ironing temperatures. Wool tends to shrink and therefore is usually dry-cleaned. Some silks are very fragile and will spot or discolor if they are washed improperly. Fabrics that have been colored with fugitive dye stuffs (*fugitive* means they will bleed and discolor other fabrics) must be dry-cleaned. Carefully read the care label that is sewn into each garment before you make your purchase and decide if the use of the garment will be compatible with the care you will have to give it.

Leather is increasingly popular as a clothing material. Leather is expensive to begin with, and maintaining it adds even more to the cost. Because it may fade when cleaned, it is often re-dyed as a part of the cleaning process. Leather pants stretch and often have to be altered after frequent wear. Leather combined with fabric in a garment may limit the way the garment can be cleaned. Consider these maintenance costs carefully when purchasing a leather garment.

Structured garments must usually be dry-cleaned because many different fabrics are used in their construction. The outer fabric, lining, interfacings, and padding may all have slightly different care instructions. Dry cleaning is the only process that would be suitable for all of them.

Knits may be made from any fiber and in a variety of weights, textures, and patterns. A well-constructed knit has stretch and recovery so that it does not lose its original shape. The yarns should have sufficient "twist" so they do not rub and pill. Most wool sweater yarns have a good natural twist, but some of the hair yarns, like mohair, are easily damaged and subject to pilling. Nylon and acrylic yarns, especially those that have been brushed, pill easily.

Cool Weather Sweater

Year-round sweater

Summer T-shirt Knit

Cranberry

Red and White

Pink and White

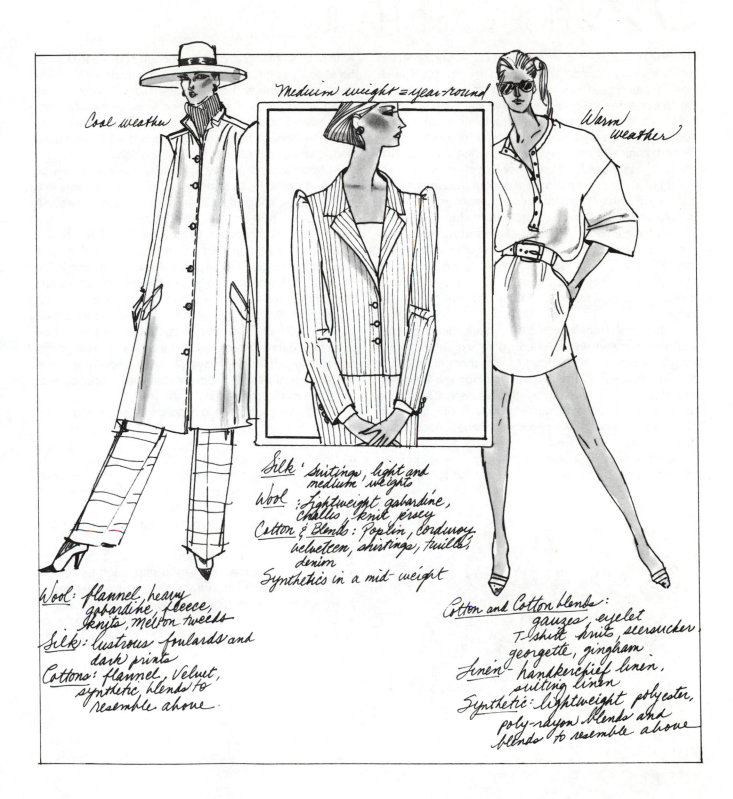

Cool weather

Medium weight = year-round

Warm weather

Silk: suitings, light and medium weights
Wool: Lightweight gabardine, challis, knit jersey
Cotton & Blends: Poplin, corduroy, velveteen, shirtings, twills, denim
Synthetics in a mid-weight

Wool: flannel, heavy gabardine, fleece, knits, Melton tweeds
Silk: lustrous foulards and dark prints
Cottons: flannel, velvet, synthetic blends to resemble above.

Cotton and Cotton blends: gauzes, eyelet T-shirt knits, seersucker, georgette, gingham
Linen: handkerchief linen, suiting linen
Synthetic: lightweight polyester, poly-rayon blends and blends to resemble above

59 WEIGHT AND HAND

The weight of a fabric is an important consideration, especially when a durable garment is being purchased. Heavier fabrics, suitable for pants, skirts, and jackets, are called *bottom weights*. *Blouse weights* are lighter fabrics best used for tops and dresses. The fabric weight should suit the garment style and the season for which it is intended. Winter fabrics are usually heaviest, spring fabrics are a medium weight, and summer fabrics are the lightest weight of all. To get the most out of your wardrobe, select as many medium-weight fabrics as possible and use them in layers to adapt them to temperature changes.

Tailored garments, such as jackets and coats, must be made in a fabric that is heavy enough to support the tailored details. If the fabric is too thin, seams will show through when they are pressed, pockets will show as ridges in the shell fabric, and bound buttonholes will be lumpy.

Light, transparent fabrics often require a lining or a full slip, which makes the garment more expensive. Light-weight fabrics can be bonded to give them greater bulk and substance. A thin layer of fabric or foam is laminated (glued under pressure and heat) to the wrong side. The fabric and the bonding material may separate during cleaning or washing if the bonding process is poorly done or the wrong glue is used.

Hand refers to the feel of the fabric. Hand can be altered greatly by the kind of finish applied to the fabric.

A crisp finish may give a fabric enough body so that it can be used as a bottom weight. The same fabric with a dress finish will be soft and drape more fluidly. Finishes break down when pressed, cleaned, or worn. Generally, less-expensive fabrics are finished to create a crisper hand and more body. A well-constructed fabric will have natural body that will not require excessive finishing.

A fabric's hand greatly influences the way it can be styled. A primary rule of design is to style garments in a fabric that is compatible with the silhouette desired. A fabric that is fluid and soft cannot be used for a crisp, well-tailored garment such as a blazer. The silhouette will reflect the body shape if a fabric with a soft hand is used. A fabric that drapes well will fall gracefully and cling to the figure. More gathering can be used with a soft fabric, and the garment will not become bulky, puffy, or awkward. A crisp fabric, like linen or sailcloth, can be used for a well-defined, tailored silhouette. A stiff interfacing would be used to add more structure to areas such as collar, cuffs, and placket. Interfacing may be used in draped garments, but a very light weight is appropriate to be compatible with the hand of the soft fabric.

Some adjectives used to describe fabric hand and texture are:

- *Dry.* Grainy, resilient texture, typical of linen.
- *Slick or wet.* Slippery texture, typical of acetate surah.
- *Crisp.* Characteristic of a sized (starched) fabric such as organdy or silk organza.
- *Boardy.* Stiff fabric; a derogatory term for a cheap fabric with too much sizing.
- *Gutsy.* Fabric with much body.
- *Lofty.* Fabric with a high pile or nap, such as velvet.
- *Flat.* Weave with low surface interest, such as poplin.
- *Rough.* Heavily textured surface, such as raw silk.
- *Crepy.* Light-textured surface, typical of crepe de chine.

Lofty Fabric   *Flat Fabric*

Pearl grey

Soft

Tailored

Silver

Pearl grey

Marigold

139

60 PATTERN: SCALE

Taste in patterns to adorn the body is as individual as fingerprints, and there is no absolute right or wrong to their selection. Taste develops as you grow. A favorite garment in childhood may inspire a fondness for a special kind of pattern. Ethnic and geographical origins influence pattern preference. Exposure to art trends, interior design, and other visual stimuli modifies taste. Taste is a result of unconsciously analyzing all the sensory input accumulated during a time period and applying it to specific choices of colors or patterns in apparel and home furnishings.

Scale means the size of the pattern. A pattern should be compatible in scale with the garment it is made into and with the size of the wearer. A large, dramatic print would be effective on a simple architectural garment or one that has a great deal of fabric. A large print on stiff fabric seems bolder than on soft fabric. For example, chiffon prints are often very large, but because of the transparency and fluidity of the fabric, the impact of the print is softened. A dramatic print that is large or colored in bold contrasts can be beautiful if the garment is designed to show the print off effectively, if the wearer wants to stand out, and if the wearer can carry it.

A petite woman will be overpowered by a large, boldly colored print. Such a pattern is best worn by larger women. A large print that is softly colored in neutrals or harmoniously blended shades is more versatile. It does not have the power of bold coloring, yet still can have a great deal of impact. It would be a good choice for a shorter person who wants to dress dramatically.

Small-scale prints are more versatile. They can be worn by petite as well as large women. A closely spaced print will seem more like a tone of color than a collection of individual motifs. Prints that consist of small, definite, widely spaced motifs look out of scale on a large woman. The eye tends to register unconsciously the number of designs it takes to cover the body, so the bulk of the person's body is emphasized by the small unit of the print.

Patterns that have the effect of textures rather than distinct print units are effective on many figure types. These include moiré patterns, tweeds, light plaids, houndstooth, small ginghams, small dots, and fine stripes. These motifs are "no-pattern patterns"; like closely spaced prints, they create the illusion of soft color.

Evaluate how a print looks by shopping carefully. Try on the garment in a large, well-lit dressing room, and stand back from the mirror to evaluate the entire effect of the garment. Wear makeup that is strong enough to balance the effect of bold colors, if that is your choice. Step 3 feet away from the mirror, and check to see if the print is so large and bold that it detracts from your face. Then evaluate the effect of the garment 10 feet from the mirror and then at 20 feet or more. Beware of spots of color that emphasize unflattering parts of the anatomy. The garment that successfully passes this careful test will be a good choice.

This bold, high contrast pattern would be best on a larger woman.

This softly colored print on chiffon could be worn by petite, as well as average or tall women.

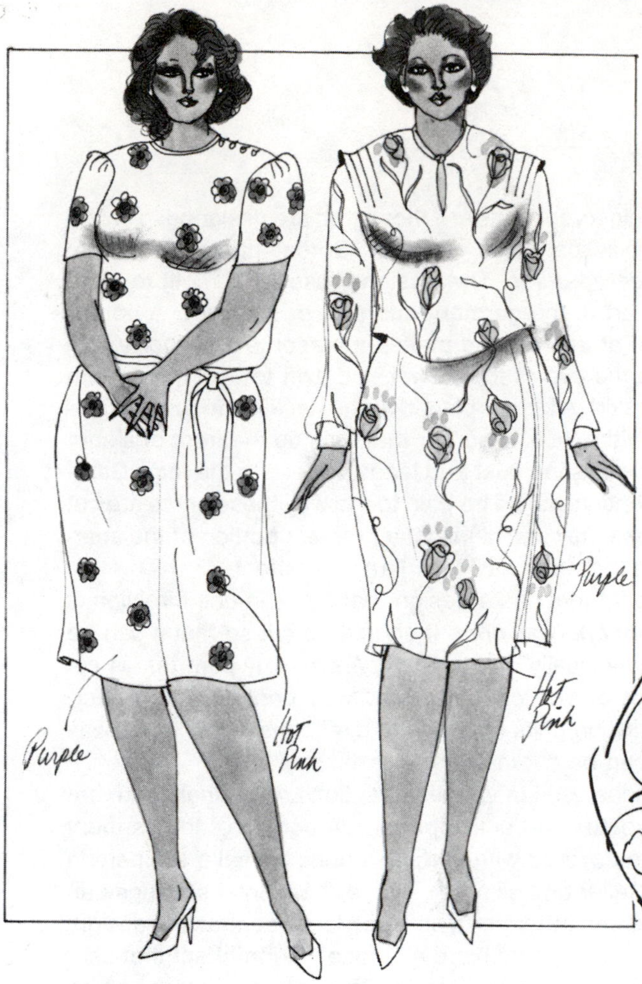

The small, spaced patterns make a heavy person seem larger. A soft all-over print is more flattering to a large figure because it does not define the space as specifically.

Purple

Hot Pink

Purple

Hot Pink

Subtle combination of Purple and Magenta

61 PATTERN MOTIFS

Pattern motifs can originate from many sources. Nature is one of the primary sources for print inspiration. Flowers, leaves, animals, and other natural objects are stylized, simplified, and combined in an infinite variety of ways. The imagination of the artist can provide a wealth of ways to arrange geometric shapes into prints and patterns such as stripes, plaids, and checks. Many geometric patterns spring from the rich tradition of woven textiles. They are created by the constraints of a loom and the typical crossing of yarns in a square or twill pattern.

Almost any object or symbol—machines, maps, letters—can be interpreted in the light of modern times and current artistic trends and transformed into a pattern motif. Logos did not enter the apparel market with the popularity of designer names and initials. Every royal family had a coat of arms that contained stylized elements that symbolized their family. The fleur-de-lis is an example of a symbol that has been used by artists and designers in many periods and places.

Embroidered surfaces provide pattern for fabric. These include appliqués, embroidery stitching, and the interweave of threads for a fabric like lace. The patterns created by any of these techniques range from free form and fanciful to disciplined and geometric. Monotone embroidery is subtle and delicate with a feminine look. Colorful, ethnic embroidery works like a printed pattern.

Engineered prints are those that are designed to fall on a specific part of a garment. Border prints are typical engineered prints. The designer uses this motif to highlight part of the garment and part of the body. A border placed at the hemline makes a person seem shorter because the eye of the viewer is drawn toward the bottom of the skirt. A border placed at the neckline focuses attention on the face. A border that runs up the front of a shirt emphasizes the bust and leads the eye to the face. Careful attention should be paid to the way these prints are cut because they can highlight a problem portion of the anatomy rather than having a flattering effect.

A print that has a design that faces in one direction is called a *one-way print*. It should be cut so that it can be viewed logically on the body. A one-way print that is cut "upside-down" looks peculiar. Most print designers alternate design units in opposite directions. Such a two-way print can be cut in either direction.

Stripes used in various directions on a single garment can create an effective pattern. A portion of the garment can be covered with vertical stripes to make the person seem taller and slimmer: bias or horizontal stripings can be used on other parts as a border or contrasting design.

Bayadère prints have a "loose" stripe effect that usually runs across the fabric. This stripe effect must be planned carefully because it is often so subtle that the stripes are visible only from a distance. The effect could enlarge or focus attention on an unfortunate part of the body.

One-Way Print

Two-Way Print

Bright Primary Colors

Red Trim

Red

Black and White

Black and White

White

White

Embroidery can also act as a print. A border print used vertically will enhance
height. Stripes can create patterns if used in different directions.

62 PATTERNED FABRICS

There are several excellent esthetic reasons to wear patterned fabrics. One of the most important is prints can camouflage a figure problem by providing textural and pattern interest that detracts from the size and shape of the body. A second important reason is that they provide pattern and colors that can coordinate solid-colored pieces of an outfit and pull together unusual color combinations. A final reason, and probably the most important one for selecting a print, is that you find it appealing and want to use it to decorate your body.

Consider the fabric that the print is on after deciding whether the pattern and color is flattering. Certain prints are typical of certain fabrics. Calico prints, for example, are traditionally printed on smooth cottons and are appropriate for warm-weather garments and children's wear. Calicos have a naive, country look and are printed in primary brights or soft neutrally tinted florals. Foulards and paisleys are favorite motifs that look well on a variety of base goods, from silk to wool challis to informal cotton. A subtle print can look dismal on a matte fabric with no natural luster. The same print will be sophisticated and lustrous when printed on a rich silk or silklike synthetic.

The blend of colors in a print can be used to pull two solid garments together. The "weight" or overall coloration of the print should be softer or slightly lighter than the solid colors that it is worn with. Distance is the most effective way for evaluating the compatibility of prints and solids in your wardrobe. Do the colors blend well? Is one piece of the outfit so bold that it fights the two subtler elements? This is usually an easier evaluation to make if you are not wearing the clothes, because your personality is not a part of the evaluation. As we have said before, never match prints and solids by looking at small pieces of the fabrics. Colors may seem compatible close up but be very different from afar. Even experienced apparel designers hang their outfits around them and study them to determine the visual compatibility of their components.

Patterns acquire a personality when made up into a specific garment. Fashion often decrees a specific type of pattern for a specific kind of apparel. For example, a small- to medium-sized monotone in neutrals or medium brights looks matronly when cut into a garment for a large, mature figure and matched with conservative pants and jackets. The same pattern in a small, trim garment designed for the junior market may have a totally different personality.

Public appearances, in front of a large group or on television, require an especially careful selection of apparel. Prints are often difficult to wear in these situations because they either appear faded from a distance or are so bold that they detract from your words and personality. Dress in several outfits and test them yourself before you decide on an outfit for a public appearance. Remember that you want to look chic, in control of the situation, and appropriately dressed for the occasion. Your outfit should only set the stage for your words and personality. Too bold an outfit or one element of it will distract the attention of your audience and render your words ineffective.

Grey
Red

Good dress print but difficult to match to solid colors

Red
Grey
White
Black

Good blouse print because of many combinations possible

Cream

Burgundy, Cream and Navy

Beige Ground

Navy

Burgundy

Navy

Cream

Prints and patterns break up the space on a figure and can camouflage some figure problems if the print is appropriate.

63 PATTERN COMBINATIONS

Combining two patterns in one outfit is more difficult to do successfully than combining plain and patterned fabrics. Patterned surfaces are a more complicated mix.

Here are some guidelines for the successful combination of patterns.

1. Choose patterns that are unified by color and design. An effective combination is the use of positive and negative versions of one pattern. A positive print is one in which a colored design is printed on a white or light-colored ground. A negative print of the same pattern simply reverses the coloring—the light color is used for the design, and the original design color becomes the ground. The unity of color and motif and the elements of contrast work to create an interesting yet controlled combination.

2. The patterns may be different but should be compatible. There is no right or wrong formula for this. The talented designer can select a small pattern that is relief for a large, bold design. The small pattern might be used on the trim and details of the garment as a contrast to the larger print. It is most important that these patterns be colored in a related scheme, either a blend of colors or a sharp contrast.

   Geometric patterns are a natural for combinations. Often stripes and dots that share colors are designed as "twin" prints.

3. The fabrics on which different patterns are printed should be compatible. The prints should be printed on similar fabric so that there are not too many diverse elements to confuse the design.

4. The different prints should not be so similar that the combination appears to have occurred by mistake instead of by design. Make sure the prints complement each other in color, motif, scale, and fabric.

An outfit of several prints can be dramatic. The tradition of the American patchwork quilt has inspired many designers. One is Koos Van Der Acker. His fanciful combinations of prints, ribbons, and laces appliquéd to base goods fabrics are works of art. Quilts have been the source of many fabric designs and are often made into specialty garments.

The combination of prints and fabrics with rich surface texture deserves the same careful attention as the combination of two prints. It is particularly important to view the combination at a distance. Multicolored textured fabrics like tweeds and textured knits take on subtle colorations that show up only at a distance.

Traditional men's wear is a mix of many patterns and

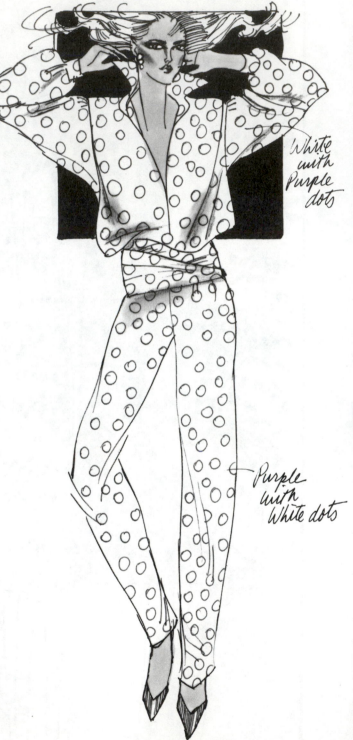

White with Purple dots

Purple with White dots

textures in one outfit—patterned suiting worn with a patterned tie and a woven shirting. Women's wear imitates this combination of tailored fabrics in a style called the *haberdashery look.*

cream

Red

Chocolate, Red, and Grey Tweed

Rust, brown and cream

Brown and rust

Magenta

Rust

Dark Chocolate

Rust

Chocolate with red plaid

chocolate

Wearing several patterns in combination calls for sophistication and careful selection.

Undergarments are called *foundations* because they shape or contain parts of the body and effect the way clothes worn over them look. A slim, active body with a youthful, uplifted bosom needs only a few, lightweight foundations. Problem figures need well-fitted foundations designed to minimize the problems. Corrective foundations are important for heavier figures and to balance underendowed figures.

The bra is the most important foundation for a woman with a large bust. A bra should fit the rib cage snugly. A bra that is too tight will force flesh into an unsightly roll; a bra that is too loose will not support the bosom. The back strap should align with the base of the bosom around the body and not hike up. Tightening the shoulder straps too much will pull the back strap up rather than raising the bust, because the bust has a natural level that cannot be substantially altered. When the straps of a bra lose their elasticity, replace the bra. The cup should be filled with no excess bulge at the cleavage.

Wash your bras in mild suds and air dry them because detergents and high heat from a dryer shorten the life of the elastic. Perspiration also attacks the elastic in a bra and should be removed regularly.

Select bras that are close to your skin color. Colored or white bras may be attractive when worn alone, but they tend to show through clothes. Undergarments should not be seen—only their effects are important.

To put your bra on properly, bend over from the waist, and let your bosom fall naturally into the cups of the open bra. Snap the bra closed and stand up. Your bust should feel contained and comfortable in a brassiere that is the proper size.

There are many different kinds and cuts of bras. The two main types are minimizers, which are styled to fit very large bosoms, and maximizers, which add fullness to a small bust. Women with a large bosom must pay the greatest attention to the fit and style of their foundation. Several specialists construct minimizers. Berlé, Edith Lance, Bali, Warners, and Lily of France are some. A minimizer is cut with a wider cup that spreads the flesh to the side instead of projecting it forward. A wider shoulder strap is generally necessary to give more support, to take some of the pull from the front and the back of the torso, and to ease the pull on the shoulder. Straps may be cushioned for added comfort. A bra that closes in the back is best for a full bosom. For a strapless bra, a full figure should select a long-line bra that comes to the waist because it gives more support and control. The minimizers are often boned or wired for additional support.

The woman with a small or average bosom has a greater variety of bra styles to choose from. Underwire bras are also excellent for a small bosom because they have support under the bust and a smooth or ornamental cup but no extra bulk or wide support straps. Maximizer bras may have a fiber-filled cup to fill out the entire bust area. Small pads under the cups also enhance a bosom.

The natural look is important in foundations today. The bra cup should have a natural, rounded shape that reflects the bust shape and avoids any pointed or artificial shapes. Seamless bras provide a smooth underlayer for most clothing and are available in styles suited to most bosom sizes. Athletic bras are constructed with the extra support needed during vigorous exercise.

A kiss of death for any garment is to have a bra strap showing. Examine your outfit carefully before you leave your dressing room to make sure your bra does not show through your shell garment and that your straps don't show. If they do, change your foundation so that it remains unseen support.

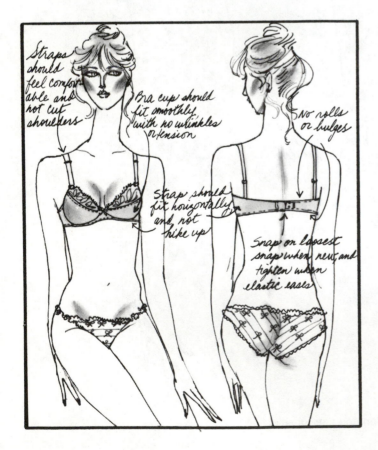

Straps should feel comfortable and not cut shoulders

Bra cup should fit smoothly with no wrinkles or tension

No rolls or bulges

Strap should fit horizontally and not hike up

Snap on loosest snap when new, and tighten when elastic eases

Proper fit for a bra.

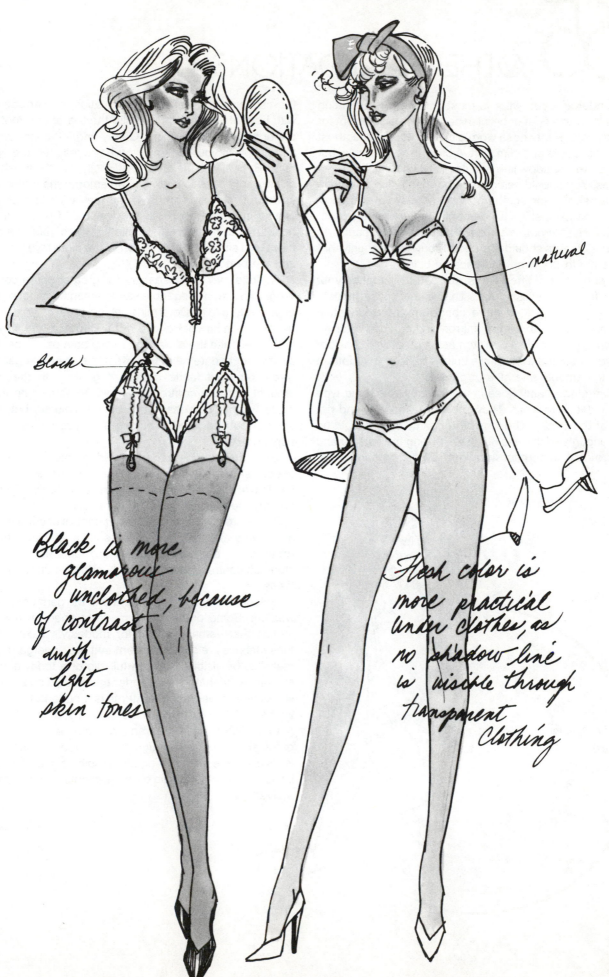

Black

natural

Black is more
glamorous
unclothed, because
of contrast
with
light
skin tones

Flesh color is
more practical
under clothes, as
no shadow line
is visible through
transparent
clothing

149

65 OTHER FOUNDATIONS

The underpant you wear is most important when fitting pants. A simple brief or bikini or panty hose is sufficient for a slim figure. Panty hose worn alone gives the smoothest line under pants or a slim skirt. A bikini is comfortable, but may cause a shadow line or a flesh line under tightly fitted clothes. You should select undergarments that are close to your skin color so there is no shadow line in light-colored pants or skirts. Underpants that are trimmed with lace may also create a shadow line under snug pants. All your underpants should fit smoothly but not so snugly that they cut into the flesh and cause a bulge.

Try on a pair of fitted pants, and carefully analyze your figure from the waist down. This is the critical test to determine if you need more control in your foundation garments. Use a three-way mirror, and pay particular attention to your derriere and stomach. You should consider additional control if there are bulges of flesh that detract from the smooth line of your pants.

Control-top panty hose is the least cumbersome type of foundation to wear. They should fit smoothly and not grab at the crotch. The legs of the panty hose should be long enough so there is no stress pulling the legs up and the crotch is in contact with flesh. To put on panty hose

for maximum comfort and preservation, gather each leg with both of your hands and slip the toe of one foot into the bottom of the stocking. Gently unroll the stocking as you pull it up your leg until you have reached the upper thigh. Repeat with the other leg. Finally, pull the waistband of the panty hose to mid-hip, and smooth the crotch area upward close to your body. You may wish to tuck your blouse in before adjusting the waistband of your panty hose at your natural waist. This will keep your blouse in place and smooth the transition of the extra layer of fabric into the bottom.

A girdle may be necessary for greater figure control. Work with a knowledgeable salesperson to select a girdle or a panty girdle. Determine which area of your figure needs the most control. Do not just look at the way the girdle fits. Take the extra time to slip on a pair of pants or a slim skirt to determine the effect that the undergarment gives the shell fabric. Select a girdle with the exact amount of figure control you need, remembering that a girdle will not decrease your overall volume, but it will smooth out the figure's bulges and give you a sleeker appearance.

Girdles should be hand washed in cold water and air dried. Use a mild soap and elastic conditioner to extend the life of the garment. Drying in an electric dryer will destroy the elasticity of a girdle rapidly.

There are a wide range of other control undergarments available that may be appropriate for a special garment. An all-in-one body smoother will provide a bra and some stomach control and is especially effective under a sleek dress.

Select slips that are appropriate to the garment you are wearing. Some dresses are made in sheer, lightweight fabrics that demand a slip for modesty's sake. Often, these fabrics are so transparent that the undergarment is meant to be visible. Select a full slip or a teddy and half slip with a cut that fits well under the dress. The color that works best under most garments is a nude that matches your skin. Wear a strapless bra so that your shoulders do not look like a mass of straps. Make sure the lower half of the slip is opaque enough so no shadow of underwear is visible. Lace trim on slips and teddies can be attractive if it is compatible with the outer garments and is appropriately placed.

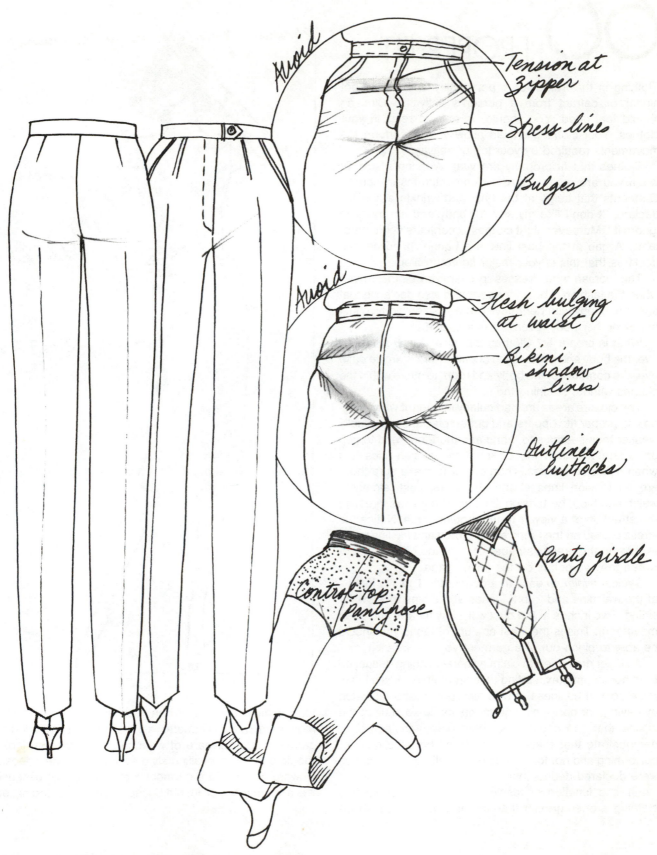

Avoid

— Tension at zipper

— Stress lines

— Bulges

Avoid

— Flesh bulging at waist

— Bikini shadow lines

— Outlined buttocks

Control top pantyhose

Panty girdle

The pant should fit without tension lines or underwear marks. The fit should be trim and not baggy in a classic trouser.

Clothing is the frame for a personality and should not hinder or detract from a person's activities. Clothing should feel good. You should be able to relax in your clothes. Your clothing should allow you to perform the movements required by your job or activity.

Clothes that fit properly are vital. Wearing a size 10 when you are really a size 12 demonstrates insecurity. Garments that bulge at the bust and wrinkle at the hip declare, "I don't like my size 12 body and am trying to ignore it." Moreover, tight clothes accentuate figure problems. A gap at the bust line is a banner headline that declares that this is your major figure problem.

The woman who dresses in oversized clothes, even when the fashion is body-conscious, is also declaring that she is unhappy with her body. The oversized clothing just hangs on her body, even if it is a size 18!

What is proper fit? Clothes that fit well flow smoothly over the body and do not cling or pull. There is ample ease over the contours of the body and room to move within the clothes without straining them.

The closure areas are particularly important when diagnosing proper fit. Zippers and button plackets are usually weaker than seams and fabric and therefore tend to gap or separate. Check the closures for tension lines first when trying on clothes. Then check to make sure there are no tension lines at the shoulders, bust, stomach, waist, and hip. The tension lines act like arrows directing the attention of a viewer to the problem area. Notice the stress placed on the fabric at the crotch and hip line in the sketch on the previous page. Look at the difference between the two outfits on the facing page.

Typical *minimum* ease in a garment is 1 to 1½ inches at the waistline and 2 to 3 inches at the hips to allow for sitting. Two inches at the bust will allow for arm and torso movement. This is the least amount of fabric you should be able to pinch out of a garment you are wearing.

A singer once tried to claim a liberal clothing deduction from her income tax, stating that her clothing was a legitimate cost of business. It was disallowed. She retaliated by having her performing garments made so snug at the hipline that she could wear them only standing up, to demonstrate that these clothes could be used only for performing and not for sitting and socializing. The clothes were declared deductible!

Fit is a function of fashion. The volume styled into clothing is often greater than the amounts set out above

Minimum comfort ease for a fitted garment

2 inches

1 to 1½ inches

2 to 3 inches

for minimum comfort. When fashion is in a cycle that requires a softer silhouette, a lot of fullness is added to garments. But, beware of wearing a garment that looks too tight for the prevailing style even if that style is loose. Beware of wearing a garment that is loose not because it is a voluminous style, but because it is simply too big on you.

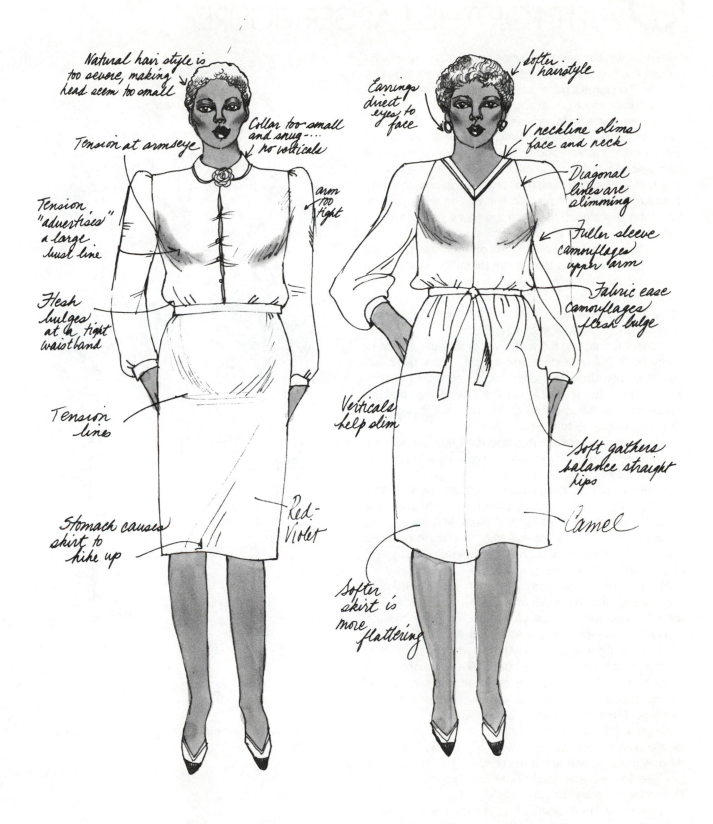

Natural hair style is too severe, making head seem too small

Tension at armseye

Collar too small and snug.... no verticals

Tension "advertises" a large bust line

arm too tight

Flesh bulges at a tight waistband

Tension lines

Stomach causes skirt to hike up

Red-Violet

softer hairstyle

Earrings direct eyes to face

V neckline slims face and neck

Diagonal lines are slimming

Fuller sleeve camouflages upper arm

Fabric ease camouflages flesh bulge

Verticals help slim

Soft gathers balance straight hips

Camel

Softer skirt is more flattering

67 FIT FOR THE LARGER FIGURE

The larger woman needs to define and slim her figure with vertical lines and not overwhelm it with flowing tunics and smocks. Too large a garment again emphasizes the figure problem instead of minimizing it.

As a woman's girth increases, the length of her garments must also increase. The greater length is needed to balance the greater width. The shoulders and bust are fuller and require more length to cover them. Check the length of a top by bending over at the waist and checking to make sure there is no skin showing at the waistline. Avoid the overblouse that cuts the figure at the midway point and reinforces the square silhouette.

The large woman should focus on the best attributes of her figure and dress to highlight them. The vertical line should be the theme of all your garments. Your clothes should fit the contours of your body. Stress lines must be carefully avoided, but a slim silhouette should be created to minimize the bulk of your figure.

Thinner fabric, and more of it, will create the illusion of slimness. The fine texture and weight of the fabric will minimize bulk. Undergarments that are styled for opacity are the secret to the success of this look. Bulges that are visible through the sheer fabric will spoil the illusion that you are attempting to create.

Pants are not necessarily taboo for the larger woman. Pants must fit well to be effective. Avoid knits that are so soft that they cling to the bulges of your thighs and stomach. Avoid elasticized waistbands that are the signature of the pull-on pant. Instead, select pants that have a smooth waistband in the front and elastic in the back. This will allow you to wear blouses tucked in and still have the comfort of a stretch waistband. Select a straight leg pant or one with a slight flare.

Remember the television series "Maude"? Bea Arthur is a large, attractive woman who was carefully dressed for the cameras. Her successful formula was soft blouses tucked into smooth pants and slim or A-line skirts, covered with a three-quarter length vest or slim tunic. This outfit is illustrated on the next page. Many variations are possible on this formula that stresses the vertical and successfully camouflages the derriere and the waist, two usual trouble spots for the large woman.

Coats are most effective if they are full length, that is, long enough to cover all the skirts in your daytime wardrobe. A princess line and a flattering V neckline will lead the eye to the face and emphasize length. The coat should be in neutral or dark tone.

Long skirts are flattering. If your legs are slim, use a side or front slit to emphasize the verticality of the outfit. Wear a jacket that comes to the upper hip area with a long skirt, and make sure that the fabric is not too bulky. Avoid additional bulk by eliminating bulky sweaters, thick layers of outerwear jackets, and bulky furs.

Too much fullness will make a large person seem even larger.

Jewelry should focus attention on beautiful hands or a pretty face or handsome shoulders. Make sure that the jewelry is large enough so that it does not look too small against the volume of your figure but not so large that it exaggerates the size of the body.

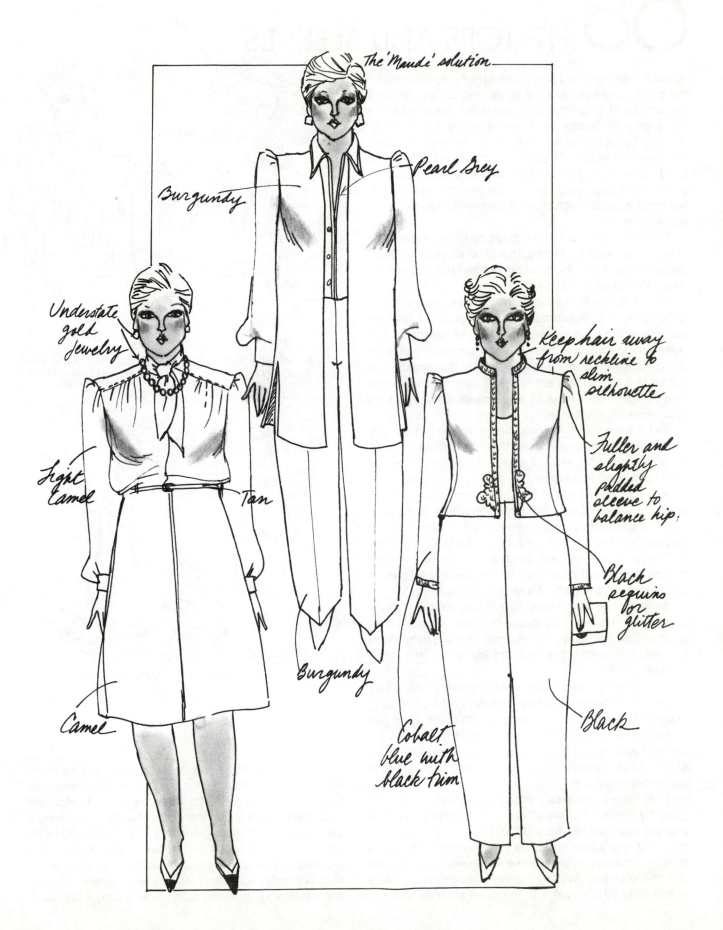

The 'Maude' solution

Burgundy

Pearl Grey

Understate gold jewelry

Keep hair away from neckline to slim silhouette

Light Camel

Tan

Fuller and slightly padded sleeve to balance hip.

Black sequins or glitter

Camel

Burgundy

Cobalt blue with black trim

Black

Apparel manufacturers make garments cut specifically for the petite, average, and full figure and for the different proportions of the junior and missy figure. But even within these general categories, fit varies widely. Every manufacturer has a different "ideal" type. Find the manufacturer whose products fit you the best. Shop stores with a good selection of your kind of merchandise. If you have a problem figure, shop early in the season because you will need a greater selection of garments than the average-size woman.

Evaluate each top you purchase carefully, especially if you are overweight. Clothing should be altered as little as possible, and tops, especially structured jackets, are the most difficult garment to alter.

The style and fit of a sleeve is the most important part of selecting a top appropriate for your figure. A full sleeve can camouflage an overweight arm, but too much fullness, due to style or a loose fit, adds too much bulk to be flattering. A sleeve that has a fuller cut at the armhole and tapers to a slim wrist is an excellent way to slim the arm. The diagonal inset lines of a wedge-shaped raglan will also minimize a full bust.

The traditional full kimono sleeve pictured at the bottom of the facing page creates few fit problems and successfully camouflages a full arm or ample bust. The tapered wrist is most flattering for the larger woman.

A set-in sleeve has a shoulder seam that joins the separate piece of fabric that forms the sleeve to the bodice. It is the most popular sleeve style. It is a flattering sleeve for a heavier figure if it fits properly. It should not pull under the arms, and there should be ample ease around the arm. It may have to be specially tailored to accommodate the girth of a very heavy arm.

Beware of wearing a short sleeve that abruptly cuts the upper arm. This line will broaden the look of a top on any but the slimmest figure. The sketch on the top right shows two ways to soften this line and make the arm seem slimmer.

Sleeveless garments are difficult to wear when your upper arm is heavy or flabby. The cut of the armhole is important. A cap sleeve widens the shoulder. This is a flattering line if you need the extra width to balance the width of your hips. The first two examples at the bottom of the page illustrate styles that camouflage a heavy upper arm effectively.

Truly bare sleeveless garments are only effective on perfectly balanced shoulders. The abrupt armhole focuses attention on the width of the shoulders and the shape of the upper arm. The cutaway armhole makes narrow shoulders seem narrower because of the diagonal line of the bodice. Wide shoulders will seem even wider in this style by contrast with the small shoulder line.

A cap sleeve is good for a full arm.

A novelty cap sleeve will balance narrow shoulders.

Sleeveless

Abrupt and unflattering, unless arms are very slim.

Makes shoulders seem wider. Only for firm arms.

Many tops are fitted with darts. Darts must fit the figure well to be effective. A dart should end slightly before the fullest part of the figure. The fullest part of the bust should be at least 1 inch above the end of the dart. Too sharp a dart line will form an awkward shape. Darts that do not fit properly focus attention on the part of the anatomy that is poorly fit. Ease, or the use of gathers and extra fabric, must fit a body curve less precisely and is a more effective and easier way to shape fabric over a body's curves.

Raglan sleeve

Unflattering, short set-in sleeve

Two solutions

The traditional Kimono sleeve is too full at the wrist to flatter a large torso.

A Kimono sleeve with a tapered wrist is more flattering

69 CONSTRUCTION: TAILORED JACKETS

The purchase of a jacket is usually a major financial commitment. You will want to evaluate the construction methods, details, and fit as well as the color and quality of the shell fabric. A well-tailored jacket will feel good when you put it on. It will hang well on your body and have substance. A well-made jacket will last for several seasons, making the time and money you invest in it well worth the reward of wearing a finely tailored garment that is appropriate for many occasions. Remember, a jacket that you pay $300 for and wear six to eight times a month is more of a value than the $150 dress you wear twice a year.

It is easier to judge the quality of a jacket if you know how it should be made. The most expensive tailored jackets are made of wool or linen and are hand constructed like a good man's suit jacket. The interlining acts as a foundation for the shell fabric. It reinforces the fabric and gives it shape. Shoulder pads add shape and allow the rest of the jacket to drape.

A constructed jacket can camouflage many figure problems because it does not cling to the body when fitted properly. The jacket should fit the body smoothly with no tension through the shoulders and midriff. The fabric should be reinforced enough so that body bulges are not visible. This fit is achieved when the garment is the proper size and has been interfaced correctly.

Traditional tailoring methods include hand "padding" many parts of the body and lapel of the jacket. Padding is the stitch that is used to connect the interlining to the top fabric of the garment. Small, well-placed stitches reinforce the shape of the jacket. Hand padding the jacket is an expensive and time-consuming process. A substitute method, called *fusing,* has been developed as a more economical alternative to hand tailoring. Interfacings are coated with a thin layer of a gluelike substance and bonded to the jacket fabric under heat and pressure. A variety of weights and types of interfacings are available.

Well-made garments have extensive interfacings fused to the body, lapel, and collar depending on the weight of the fabric and the style of the jacket. A better garment will have the same amount of fused interfacings as a hand-tailored garment has padded interfacings. As a jacket decreases in price and quality, the amount of fusing decreases because each piece that must be fused adds to the cost of the garment.

Construction details are often hidden by the lining of the garment and quality is difficult for an unpracticed eye to detect. Flip up the back of the collar and see if small stitches are visible on the undercollar. These indicate hand tailoring. Observe the stand and firmness of the collar and the roll of the lapel. There should be a softly curving roll with no breaks or buckles. The lapel should frame the face and have a balanced and graceful size and proportion. The leading edge should be straight and very flat. Check the set of the jacket (the way the garment sits on your shoulders). Evaluate the less-expensive garment with the look of the better jacket in mind. Fine tailoring and good fabric are the mark of quality in a garment, not trendy styling.

Interfacing is shown in shaded areas. It is vital to create a handsome and durable tailored jacket.

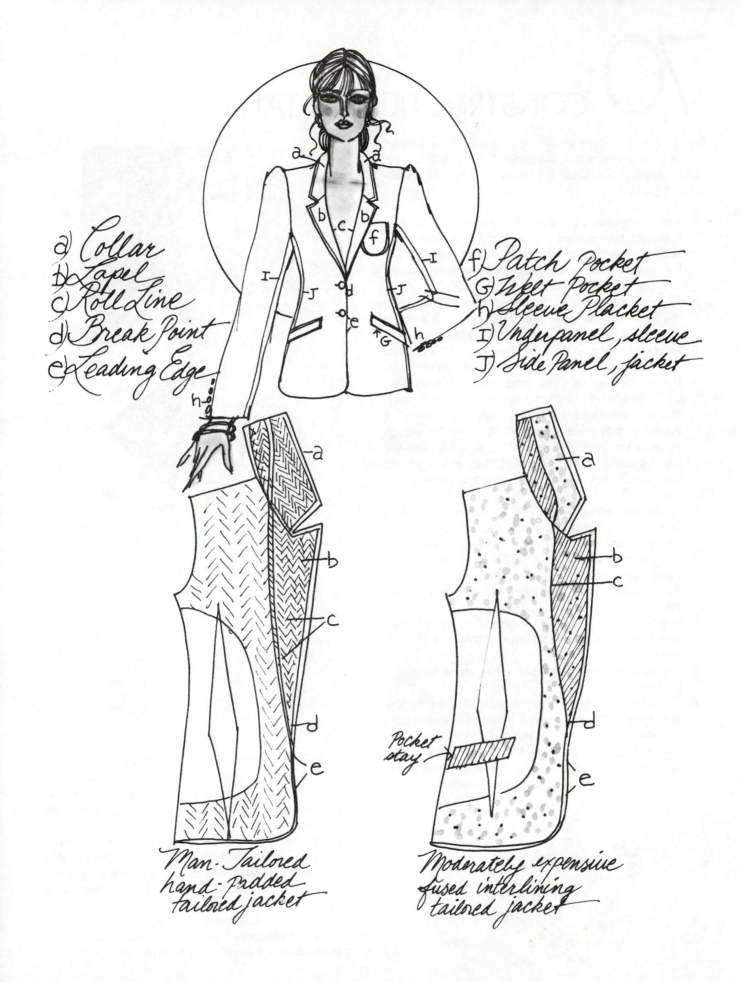

a) Collar
b) Lapel
c) Roll Line
d) Break Point
e) Leading Edge

f) Patch Pocket
G) Inset Pocket
H) Sleeve Placket
I) Underpanel, sleeve
J) Side Panel, Jacket

Pocket stay

Man-Tailored
hand-padded
tailored jacket

Moderately expensive
fused interlining
tailored jacket

Details are important indicators of quality in a tailored garment. Small parts that are perfectly sewn add up to a quality product. Look for the following things in a well-tailored garment.

1. A good shoulder pad establishes the set of the jacket. It should be squared with a rounded shoulder cap even on the hanger. An extra piece of fabric should be sewn into the armseye to round the sleeve head. The pad should be the right size.

2. There should be no hollow between the shoulder and the bust line. A smooth flow of fabric indicates fusing or a chest piece that shapes the jacket well.

3. All plackets should function. This means the buttons and buttonholes on sleeves and pockets should work.

4. Buttons should be of a good quality bone, metal, wood, or shell. Plastic buttons break and chip easily. Buttons should have a shank made out of metal or thread so they stand away from the fabric far enough to allow the other side of the jacket to be buttoned without being pulled or crushed. Buttonholes should be bound or have a rounded end with a well-stitched edge.

5. All pockets should work and be finished with shell fabric on the inner side and lining on the top side. Lining is not visible when your hand is in the pocket, and the shell fabric will sustain the wear of the pocket as the hand goes in. Lining is used on the top side of the underpocket so pocket lining does not get too thick.

6. Patch pockets should be attached to the garment securely. They should be even if they are used in pairs.

7. Top stitching should be small, even, and in an appropriate color.

8. The lining should be attached by hand at the bottom of the jacket. It should be at least an inch shorter than the shell fabric so it doesn't pull the jacket out of shape. The lining should be finished around the edge of a back vent. It should have a release pleat at the center back to allow for shoulder movement.

9. A jacket for spring and summer may be unlined. An unlined jacket should look finished when taken off. The facings should be large enough to conceal shoulder pads and interfacings. Seams should be finished in a way to prevent raveling.

10. A lining should be made of a good quality fabric in a color compatible with the shell fabric. Beware of a very stiff or heavy lining. It may be used to give the shell fabric more guts, indicating that the fabric is of inferior quality.

11. Any hidden snaps used on a jacket should be covered with a piece of lining fabric the same color as the jacket so there is no metalic glare.

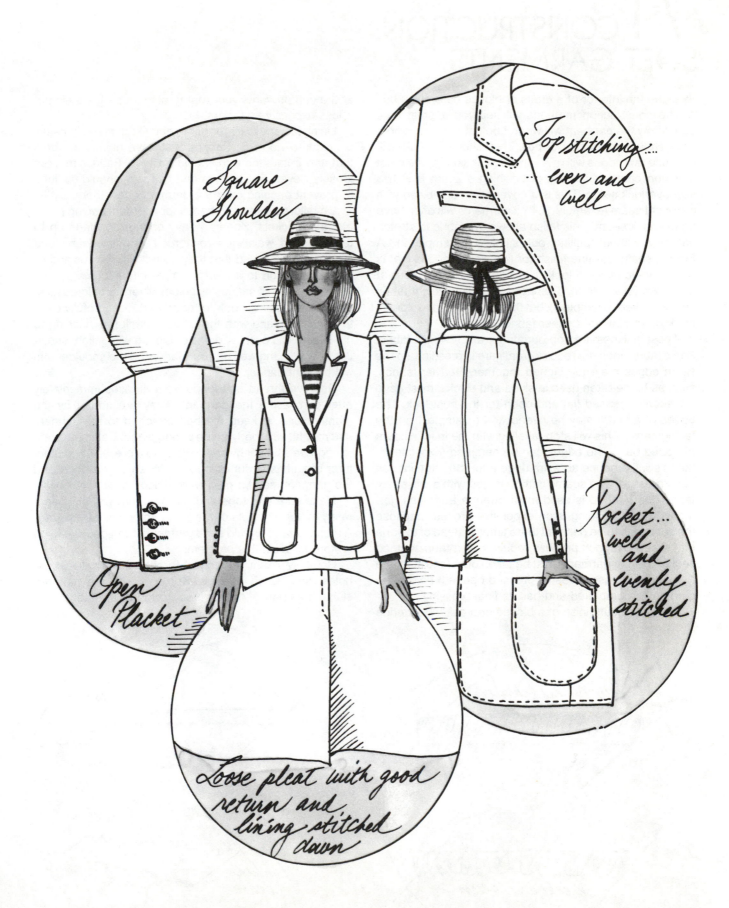

Square Shoulder

Top stitching...
...even and well

Open Placket

Pocket...
well and evenly stitched

Loose pleat with good return and lining stitched down

71 CONSTRUCTION: SOFT GARMENTS

Examine the interior of a dress or blouse before you buy it. The construction methods will tell you a great deal about how the garment will wear. Look at the seams first. They should not pucker or pull. They should be finished, because raw edges will ravel and look unsightly. The most common commercial way of finishing a seam is with a sew-overlock seam. This is a cover stitch combined with a straight seam (example 1). Knit garments will often have an overlock seam. This finish allows the fabric to stretch naturally without pulling out stitches (example 2). A French seam is a fine finish for lightweight goods that is expensive to make. It looks like a narrow tube of fabric at the seam (example 3). The edges of a lightweight fabric can be pinked (example 4), but this will often leave a press mark or shadow in a sheer fabric.

These finishes are appropriate for a lightweight fabric. A thin fabric does not require great care in pressing, so the seam edges may be stitched together. Heavier fabrics, such as those often used in skirts and slacks, must have the seams pressed flat and open for the best look. The edges of a seam may be overlocked (example 1 on the facing page). This will stop raveling with the least amount of added bulk. The edges can be hemmed (example 2), but this will produce an extra ridge after the garment has been pressed. The seams can be edged with a thin seam tape. This method is used most often in European garments. Edge finishing is an expensive process because the seam has to be handled three times instead of the one that a sew-overlock process requires, and then seamed sections of the garment must be taken out of the machine to be underpressed (seams pressed opened) before the garment is completed and has its final pressing.

Check the cuff finish of a blouse or dress. A raw edge at the cuff prevents you from turning it up. It is a sign of a less-expensive garment.

Lining is necessary for pants and skirts made in heavy or textured woolens. Fabrics that have blends of fibers that may irritate the skin should be lined. Fabrics that are loosely woven, like tweeds and flannels, should be lined to prevent bagging after the garments have been sat in.

On tailored skirts and pants, look for functioning pockets and plackets, zippers heavy enough to stand up to tension, and waistlines reinforced with interlining and inner construction so that they do not roll. Seams should be wide enough to allow for simple alterations.

Apply some of the quality guides given for tailored jackets to soft clothes. Look for good buttons, carefully dyed to match or blend with the fabric. Check top stitching to make sure it is even. A dress or blouse with a light shoulder pad will hang well on your body, and the shoulder pad will prevent hanger wear.

Remove thread belt loops from dresses immediately after purchasing the garment. They are added by the manufacturer to keep the belt attached to the garment and may hit your body at the wrong place. Do not hesitate to upgrade a belt or buttons if you like a dress. A manufacturer often has to cut corners on these accessories, and the garment may be greatly enhanced by a richer belt.

Make sure that tops and bottoms that you buy separately match. Dye lots of the same color can vary slightly. A manufacturer should send garments from one dye lot to a store to avoid this problem.

Carefully examine fabrics for flaws such as slubs, holes, and pulled threads. Some fabrics are naturally slubbed as part of the surface design of the fabric.

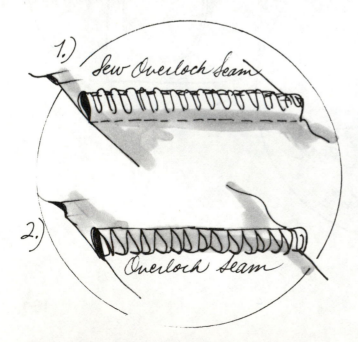

1.) Sew Overlock Seam

2.) Overlock Seam

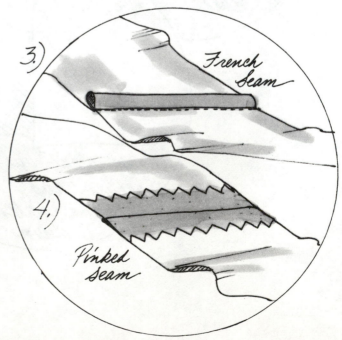

3.) French Seam

4.) Pinked Seam

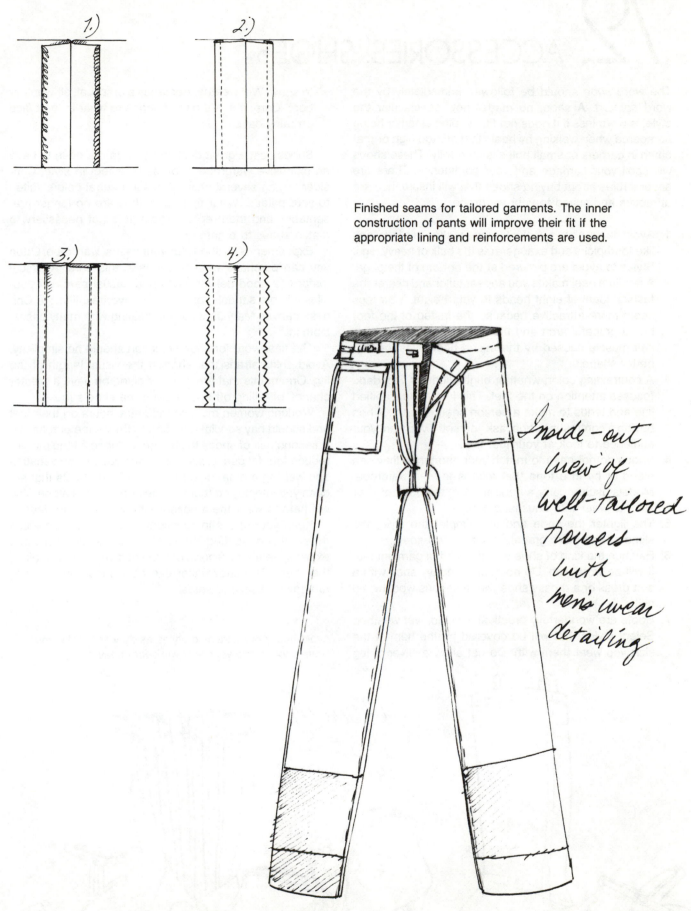

1.)

2.)

3.)

4.)

Finished seams for tailored garments. The inner construction of pants will improve their fit if the appropriate lining and reinforcements are used.

Inside-out view of well-tailored trousers with men's wear detailing

The word *shoe* should be followed immediately by the word *comfort*. A shoe, no matter how spectacular the style, is worthless if it does not fit. Limping along or being hampered when walking by heels that are too high or that catch in carpets or small holes is pure folly. These shoes will spoil your carriage and your confidence. There are several rules about buying shoes that will insure they are attractive and suited to your wardrobe.

1. Avoid heavy shoes. A clunky shoe makes thin legs look like toothpicks and exaggerates the bulk of heavy legs. Styles to avoid are pictured at the bottom of the page.

2. A medium heel makes you appear taller and nearer the fashion ideal of eight heads to your height. Your legs seem more attractive because the instep of the foot has a graceful arch and the slight contraction of the calf muscle caused by the raised heel gives the calf better shape.

3. A contrasting color, whether bright, light, or very dark, focuses attention on the feet. This interrupts a unified line and tends to make a person seem shorter. When buying a contrasting shoe, ask yourself if you want your audience to look at your feet first.

4. Shoes do not have to match your garments; they can blend or be in a tone that relates to your wardrobe. Models usually carry a neutral shoe, the color of their skin, to wear with unusual colors.

5. The lighter the shoe and the simpler the style, the slimmer and more graceful your leg will seem.

6. Balance the kind of shoe with the kind of garment that it will be worn with. Do not team a heavy shoe with a soft dress or a dressy shoe with a serious wool tweed suit.

7. Boots are wonderfully practical for cold, wet weather. Select styles that will be covered by the hem of the skirt you wear them with. Do not allow a sliver of leg to show. Wet weather demands a practical, all-weather boot. Carry a spare pair of shoes to wear in the office on rainy days.

Shoes cost a great deal, but you do not need to have an extensive wardrobe to dress your feet in style. Consider buying several basic shoes in neutral colors suited to your palette. Wear them until they are no longer presentable, and then replace them. It is not necessary to match shoes to a garment.

Experiment with shoes for your casual wardrobe. Often you can purchase whimsy shoes in this area. A casual loafer is a good bet for jeans and casual pants. Espadrilles, simple sandals, and classic favorites, like the Chinese canvas Mary-Jane, are appealing with many casual clothes.

The final word for shoe selection should be simplicity. Avoid ankle straps that shorten the visual length of the leg. Ornaments that are sewn or glued on have a greater chance of falling off and spoiling the shoe's looks.

Working women must spend many hours on their feet and should pay special attention to their shoe purchases. A second pair of shoes to change to during a long day will reduce foot fatigue. (This is a must if you are on vacation and walking a great deal.) Beware of high heels that seduce you into buying them on their good looks alone. You will hate to wear them because they abuse your feet.

Keep your shoes in excellent repair. A little care can renew dirty or scuffed shoes. Use fine saddle soaps and excellent leather preparations to keep your shoes looking their best. The shoemaker can do wonders in repairing run-down heels and soles.

Avoid heavy or distracting styles as they will make you seem shorter and your legs will seem heavier.

Unflattering Styles

Casual Shoes

Business Shoes

Dressy Shoes

73 ACCESSORIES: STOCKINGS

The most versatile stocking is a natural skin tone, has a nude toe, and is heelless. This stocking will slip into any shoe, with any garment, and blend into the complete outfit easily. Natural hose is a good basic for serious business clothes. Black women should select a tone that blends with and is a shade darker than their skin tone. A shade that is close to natural but does not quite make it has a strange look that should be avoided.

Colored hose can be used successfully to create some interesting illusions. The trick in selecting novelty hose is to balance your leg interest with the texture, color, and weight of your outfit. Generally, if you are wearing a dark bottom made from heavier weight fabric, you can wear a stocking in a subtle tone of the skirt. This will add to the illusion of height. A shoe in the same tone will add to the illusion.

Lighter-colored clothes and clothes in delicate fabrics look handsome with light-colored hose and a light shoe. Do not wear white stockings with a bone shoe; the shades are just off enough to seem mismatched. Avoid combining very dark shoes with off-white hose unless you are trying for an "Alice in Wonderland" look.

Avoid too exotic a color if you are dressing for serious business occasions. Florid pink, red, or purple hose will give your legs a very peculiar look. Your audience will notice your legs before they hazard a glance at your face.

Socks and stockings can also be selected for whimsical effects, especially with casual clothes. Argyle socks can tie together the patterns and colors in a flannel sporting outfit. Are you tall and slender and able to carry a fashion effect? Wear a brightly contrasting sock under your somber colored pants and team it with a sporty tie or novelty sweater vest the same accent color. Socks are practical comfort accessories, especially in cold and wet weather. One or two layers cushion an abrasive boot and provide warmth.

Tights are heavier versions of panty hose. They are comfortable during cold weather for insulating your legs under pants and skirts. They are very successful teamed with garments that have weight or texture.

The perennial basic is the nude leg look, appropriate for all occasions. Real zing can be added to an outfit with the right novelty stocking if it suits your figure type and leg shape. Let your mirror be the judge. Avoid too radical an effect, especially for business wear. Experiment with this inexpensive and interesting accessory to decide what is right for your fashion formula.

Patterned hose make an elegant accessory for evening clothes

white

red

black

white

Black

black or dark tone

dark toned

red and white stripe

red stockings

167

74 ACCESSORIES: HANDBAGS

Women who lead busy lives have little time to deal with "time-eaters" like shifting their possessions from handbag to handbag. This chore can be eliminated by selecting a bag that is appropriate for most of your daytime activities. Blend it with your selection of shoes (fashion rules no longer decree that shoes and bag have to match) and your color palette, and live with one daytime bag, day after day. Using one bag will give you the opportunity to make it an investment. Purchase a purse of excellent quality. Your handbag is a highly visible part of your total look and will definitely detract from your appearance if it is obviously inexpensive, worn out, or inappropriate.

Avoid toting around a huge purse loaded with all the gimcracks that have collected in it since it was purchased. For business women especially, this "saddle bag" detracts from a trim and professional appearance. Go through your purse now and look at all the things that have collected there. Eliminate the junk. Evaluate the makeup you carry—usually you have too much. Consolidate your credit cards and money into one simple wallet. Carry a note pad with a pencil or pen attached. Make sure all your keys are contained on one simple ring. Separate the absolutely essential things to carry in your bag. Chances are you have been toting around enough equipment to take care of your needs for a weekend, instead of for eight hours away from home base. A huge, sloppy tote labels you as disorganized when you have to dig through the debris for your pen or keys. Buy a more compact size when you get a new bag, and carry an extra tote or briefcase for papers, purchases, or extras when necessary.

Try fitting all of your necessary equipment in any bag before you purchase it. Make sure it is not distorted by what you want to carry and that it closes easily. Check the straps to make sure they are well secured to the bag as these will take the most pressure and wear. The clasp should be secure to discourage losses and theft.

A serious, tailored wardrobe will be best accessorized with a smooth leather bag in a classic shape. A shoulder strap that allows the bag to fall somewhere between the hip and the waist line is versatile and easy to carry. Often, you can find a bag in which the strap can be concealed and carried as a clutch. Select a soft, unconstructed pouch if soft clothing is more your style.

You may wish to select two bags to use during the year —one for your lighter weight and colored summer wardrobe and another for your winter wardrobe. Dressy evening clothes will require another bag. This can be a small, light pouch or clutch that will blend with your evening clothes.

Color and size are important considerations if you are selecting a bag for a problem figure. Too large a bag will overwhelm a petite person. A brightly colored bag will detract from the unity of an outfit color coordinated to maximize height. A solid color purse in the same tonal family would be more appropriate. Either a very small bag or a very large one will emphasize the bulk of a large woman. She should select a medium-sized handbag.

Leather handbags are usually an excellent investment. Select one that is leather lined for the best wear. Usually the cloth lining wears out long before the shell does. A smooth leather may be polished and refreshed, while a suede or novelty canvas will get dirtier sooner and be more difficult to maintain.

Select quality accessories for your purse. A tacky wallet that is falling apart or bulging with too many cards and papers is a poor advertisement for a chic person. Again, a wallet is something that you will have for several years if it is well made, so do not skimp on something that will reflect on your personal image every time you open your bag.

Large, sloppy handbags ruin the line of all clothing. Handbag styles should be compatible with the theme and coloring of your outfit and with your size.

75 ACCESSORIES: JEWELRY

Jewelry makes a personal statement. The kind and amount you wear says a great deal about your taste level. The business woman should pay particular attention to the jewelry she wears because it is the detail of an outfit most often "appraised" as a status badge by male co-workers.

A safe rule to follow when selecting jewelry is less is more. Think of jewelry as providing the final accent for your outfit. Avoid jewelry that clanks or seems too clunky. Jewelry should be the subtle accent that highlights a woman's good looks. Lustrous pearls at the neck and ears highlight a woman's coloring by contrasting with the skin. The subtle sparkle of trim earrings or a simple necklace dresses the basic business outfit and makes it seem finished. A suggestion of sparkle is the touch that balances dramatic evening makeup and a dramatic evening outfit.

Do not slavishly follow fashion photographs. Photographic stylists must often exaggerate accessories because the camera so reduces the impact of more subtle details. A high fashion designer often accessorizes with extra bold jewelry to make clothes "read" from the runway. The customer would not necessarily want to duplicate this look. I remember seeing stunning, large "silver" jewelry worn on heavy winter clothes in a prêt-à-porter (ready-to-wear) collection show in Paris. When I went backstage to see the clothes close up, I was amazed to see the jewelry had been made by cutting aluminum pie tins up in shreds, bending them into interesting shapes, and tying them on to the models with black ribbon!

Start selecting your jewelry from your head down. Earrings are very important if you want to highlight your face. Clip-on earrings can be annoying and cause headaches. Consider having your ears pierced for comfort and to prevent the loss of really valuable pieces.

Next move to your neck as a focal point. A woman with a large bust should not call attention to the obvious by wearing large, dangling pendants. This woman should focus attention upward by wearing jewelry that is closer to the base of the neck. Avoid wearing a choker if your neck is short or heavy.

Very large women should focus attention on the hands and face. Carefully evaluate any body jewelry before wearing it. Too small a piece may emphasize your girth, while a very large piece may make you seem overwhelming.

Your color palette will suggest the stones and metals that are most flattering to you and will blend best with your wardrobe. Gold and warm-toned metals are naturals for sunlight complexions, though antique silver is also handsome, especially when combined with ivory or warm-colored stones like amber and turquoise. Moon glow complexions look beautiful in white metals. Diamonds are attractive on everyone because they reflect light, but a mounting in the person's palette will be most flattering.

Remember that a watch should be thought of as important jewelry. Study classic styles, and select a size that is compatible with your wrist and hand size. Do not hesitate to select a man's watch if you have large wrists and hands. Again, go for quality because you will wear this accessory daily. Save your Mickey Mouse watch for casual clothes.

Jewelry is too small   *Too much jewelry*   *Tasteful selection*

Belts are a wonderfully versatile accessory for the woman with a waist and hip line that can be highlighted. This lucky person can select exotic colors and sizes and include large buckles and dangly accessories.

Unusual belts are available from many sources other than the conventional store counter. Twist two contrasting colored scarves and tie them over a basic blouse or dress to achieve an original look for casual or at-home wear. Use antique fabric, ethnic ties, leather straps (even try buckling two dog collars together!), or other found objects to make attractive accessories. Often one multicolored woven belt can work with several outfits in your wardrobe and key blouse colors into the solid base goods colors you are wearing. Belts are wonderful "collector's items" that can represent the many different places and people you have come in contact with.

The woman with a figure problem must invest more time and consideration into selecting a belt. Waistline definition can help to make her look slimmest. The trick to remember when belting a large figure is to make the belt as close to the color of the garment as possible. Remember all of the experiments you did on earlier pages coloring belts in dark colors, advancing colors, and blending colors? The figure with a solid tone of color seemed the tallest and the slimmest.

Tailored, slim belts should be a part of every woman's wardrobe. These are narrow enough to slim into belt loops and add a finish to the waistline of a tailored pant or skirt. The large woman should select blending colors and buckles made of oxidized (darkened) metal or covered in self fabric. A belt with long ends will provide a slimming vertical. A belt should never be so wide or so tight that it causes flesh to collect in a roll above it. Belts to wear with jeans are generally larger than your waist so that they ride on the upper hip instead of fitting the waist snugly.

Store your belts where they are visible and easy to pick out. Even a small collection can resemble a pile of unruly snakes if they are stored in a jumble at the bottom of your drawer or closet. Maintain your leather belts as you do your shoes. Should a favorite belt need repairs, take it to your shoemaker.

Tailored belt styles are pictured at the bottom of the page. Some more dramatic belts are pictured on the facing page.

A narrow self-belt defines the waistline without emphasizing it.

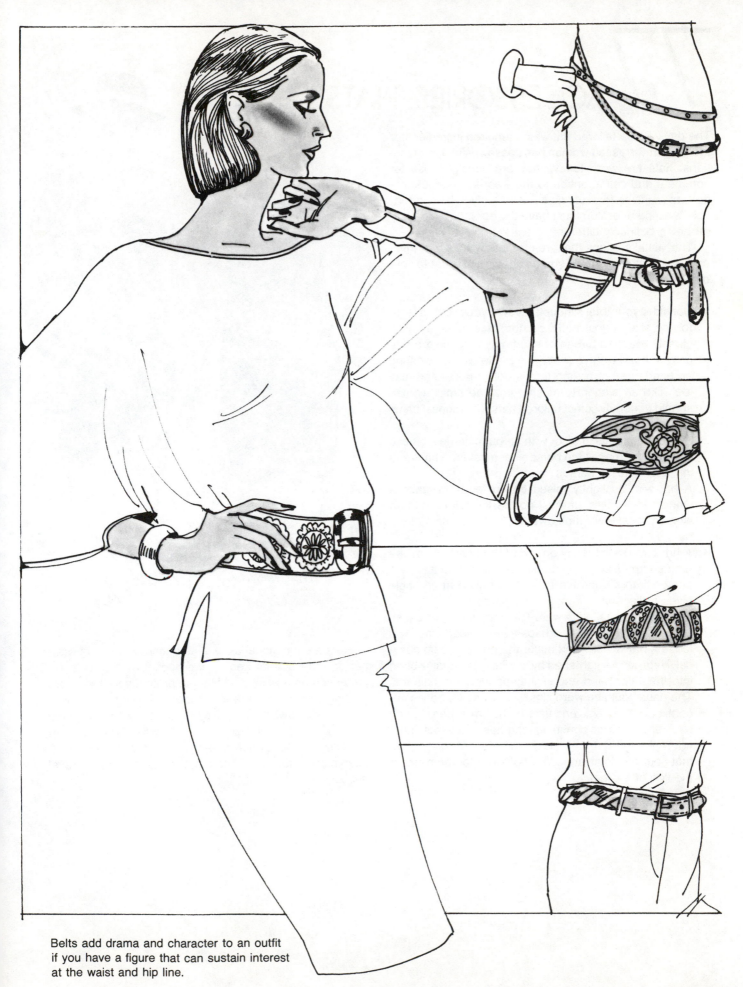

Belts add drama and character to an outfit
if you have a figure that can sustain interest
at the waist and hip line.

173

77 ACCESSORIES: HATS

The day when a tailored hat was a required ingredient for the correctly dressed woman has passed. When nonfunctional hats are worn today, they are usually cause for comment and call attention to the wearer. The most important requisite for wearing a hat is that you be comfortable wearing one. You must have the personality to carry off being definitely different.

The visual illusions that are created by hats may influence your choice, should you decide to add a hat to your outfit.

1. Consider your total silhouette first. If your head is large for the size of your body, do not select a large hat. A closely wrapped turban or scarf may balance the size of your head with your body. A petite woman wearing an overlarge hat or one that is boldly decorated may look like an elaborate mushroom. The small woman should generally select tailored hats with modest brims and crowns.
2. A hat that blends in color with an outfit carries the eye upward and makes the person seem taller. A contrasting hat makes a person seem shorter.
3. A hat with a slightly raised crown tends to make a woman look taller. (It must not be too tall for a short woman, or she will look dwarfed by the volume of the hat.)
4. A hat that sits squarely on top of the head makes the face seem fuller. This can be used to advantage by a person with a very thin face. A hat tilted at an angle gives a diagonal and more slimming line.
5. The hat should fit very well. Too snug a hat will cause some discomfort and perhaps even a headache. Too loose a hat will slip and make the person seem comical. Hats can be tightened by stitching grosgrain ribbon into the inner band and slightly padding the hatband.
6. The hair should be worn simply in a way that does not conflict with the size and flare of the hat. Often slicking back short hair or confining long hair in a simple knot will make the hat look sleek and elegant. Make sure that your hair is arranged purposefully to complement the line of the hat.

A hat in the same tone as the garment will make the person appear taller

Hats are functional as well as decorative. A soft wrap hat or beret can be kept in the pocket of your coat for protection on a rainy day. Hats to protect your face from tanning are an important outdoor accessory. Consider borrowing a cowboy hat or a pith helmet to wear for casual sunny occasions. A visor secured to the head with an elasticized band is an excellent sun hat for active wear. A scarf can be fashioned into a hat and is the perfect travel accessory.

Horizontal angle makes the face and chin seem wider

Angled hat makes face appear slimmer

Scarves are a wonderful way to focus the eye on a specific part of the body. Use a contrasting color to highlight your face by draping the scarf around your neck. Scarves can neutralize harsh clothing colors by adding a spot of your most flattering color at the neckline. Contrasting scarves at the neckline of an open blouse will emphasize the flattering V lines of the opening. A scarf makes a fine belt or even a sexy bare top.

Wrap your head in a scarf when your hair is less than presentable. Drape a large wool or silk scarf over the shoulders of a jacket or coat for added warmth and color. Use a lace hankie tucked into the pocket of a tailored suit jacket to soften the suit. Wear a long, narrow scarf, knotted at the ends to provide natural weight, around your neck when wearing a tailored suit. The natural vertical lines will enhance and slim the figure. Use a bandana tied with a perky knot as a colorful sweatband when jogging or for other active sports.

A scarf can be bothersome and fall into disarray if you do not tie it properly. Practice before wearing it to perfect your techniques. Notice how stores display scarves, and borrow their ideas. Use a small straight pin, on the underside of your garment, to pin a neck scarf to your blouse or sweater. This will prevent the scarf from slipping or coming untied as you go through the day.

Be sure to press the scarf each time you wear it. Check it for spots, and wash in mild soap or send it to the cleaners if it is soiled. Nothing is tackier than wearing a "menu"!

Scarves come in many sizes, shapes, and fabrics, each appropriate for a different application. Often designer scarves are colored in exotic prints in the colors of the season and blend well with a great many of the fashion colors used for apparel. Do not feel your scarves must all be silk. Select a scarf for color and design first. Then tie a soft knot in the scarf to make sure it has sufficient body to be tied attractively. Check the size and shape, and do a few preliminary try-on's before purchasing it. A knowledgeable salesperson will often give you important tips on new ways to wear a scarf. Cotton scarves have a wonderful look for spring and summer and are often large enough to tie into belts, hip wraps, and bare tops. A large cotton rectangle makes a wonderful summer shawl to cover up a sun dress for a casual evening.

Study the suggestions for tying and wearing scarves on this page and the next. Remember to balance the scale and intensity of this accessory to your body type and the outfit you are wearing. Adapt them to your personal style.

Vertical treatments make the face seem slimmer, and the body taller

Balanced Figure: Thin

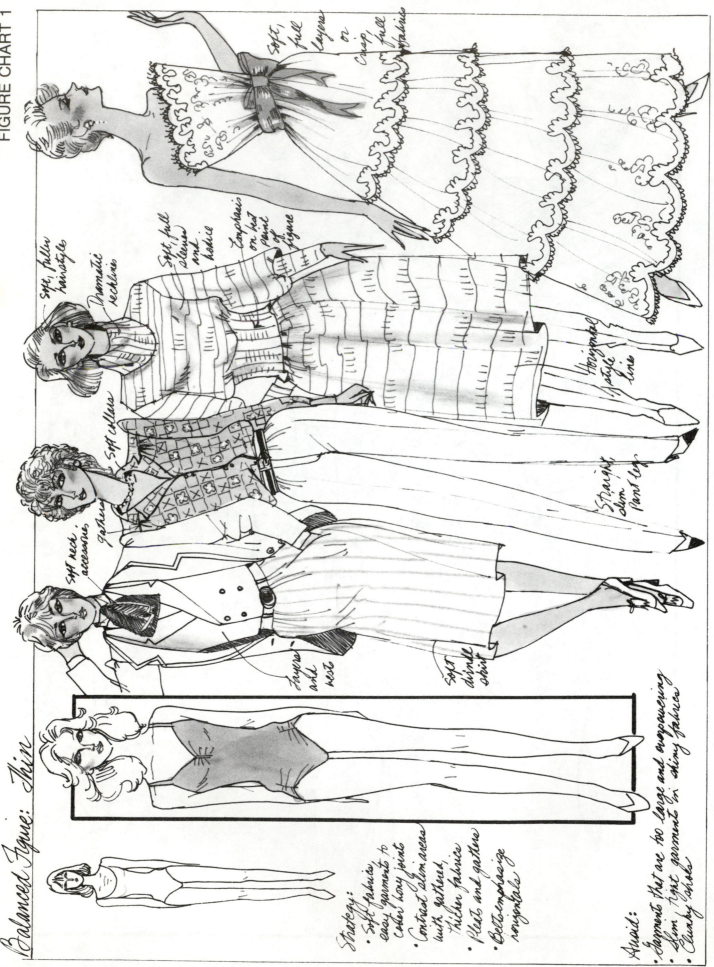

Strategy:
- Soft fabrics
- Soft garments to cover bony joints
- Contrast slim areas with gathered, thicker fabrics
- Pleats and gather
- De-emphasize nonpointed

Avoid:
- Garments that are too large and overpowering
- Slim, tight garment in shiny fabrics
- Chunky shoes

178

Balanced Figure: Average

Select dramatic colors.

Soft, dramatic dresses — To emphasize slim line

Dramatic and body-conscious clothes.

Fitted or double breasted o.k.

Dramatic Tops o.k.

Slim to full, and dramatic skirt

Slender Pants or Trousers

Great range of clothing and accessories possible.

Strategy:
• Easiest figure to dress.
• Height will determine how dramatic fashion can be worn.

Balanced Figure: Large

Strategy:
- Emphasize verticals
- Balance head size with a soft medium-volume hairstyle
- Use diagonal line
- V necklines

Avoid:
- Horizontal style lines
- Curved lines
- Too much fullness
- Too many details

Contained hairstyle

Padded shoulder to balance hip

accentor V to face

lightweight fabric

Slim silhouette

Simple, curved details

Vertical style line

Add height

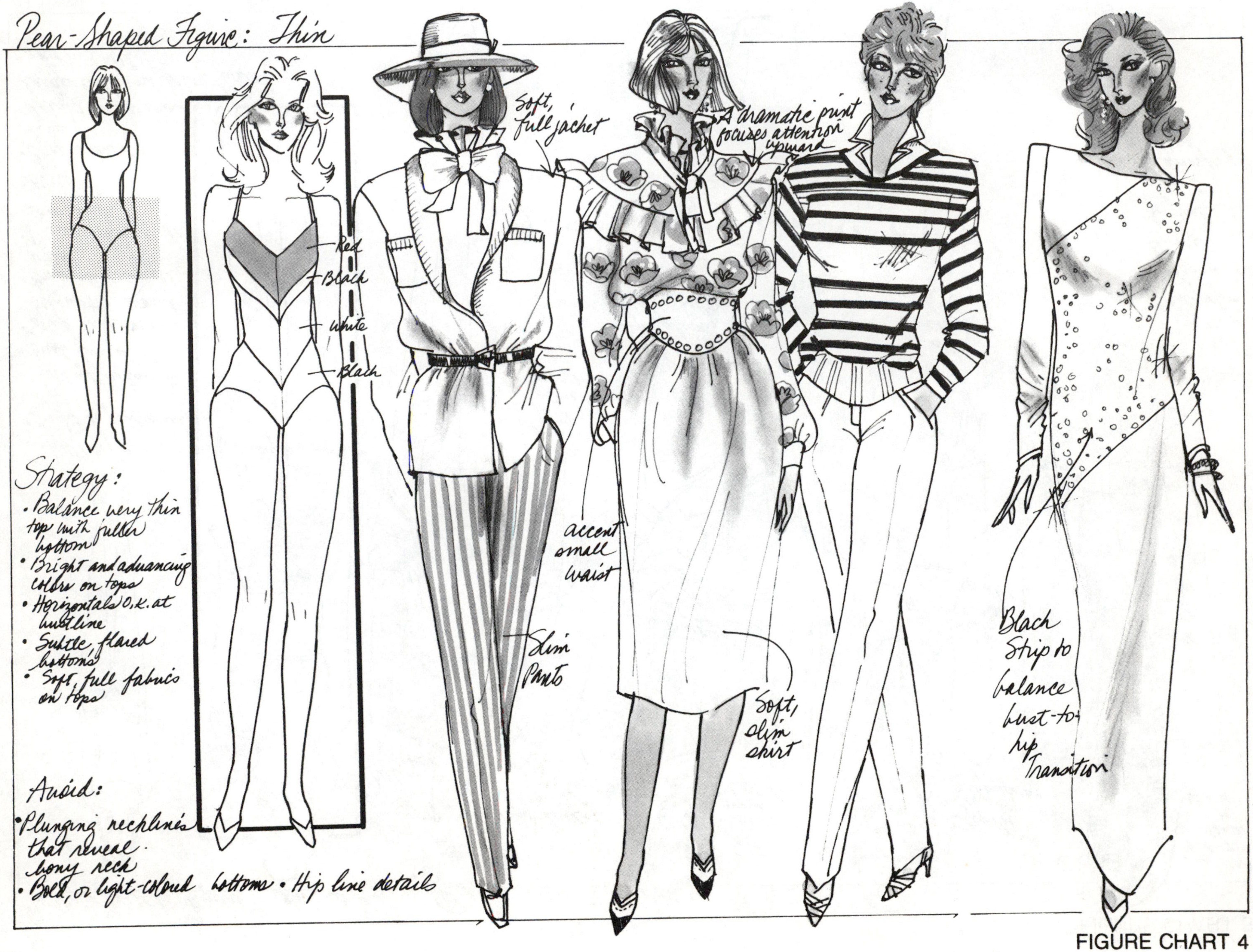
Pear-Shaped Figure: Thin
Strategy:
• Balance very thin top with fuller bottom
• Bright and advancing colors on tops
• Horizontals O.K. at bustline
• Subtle, flared bottoms
• Soft, full fabrics on tops
Avoid:
• Plunging necklines that reveal bony neck
• Bold, or light-colored bottoms • Hip line details
Red
Black
White
Black
Soft, full jacket
Slim Pants
accent small waist
A dramatic print focuses attention upward
Soft, slim skirt
Black Strip to balance bust-to-hip Transition

FIGURE CHART 4

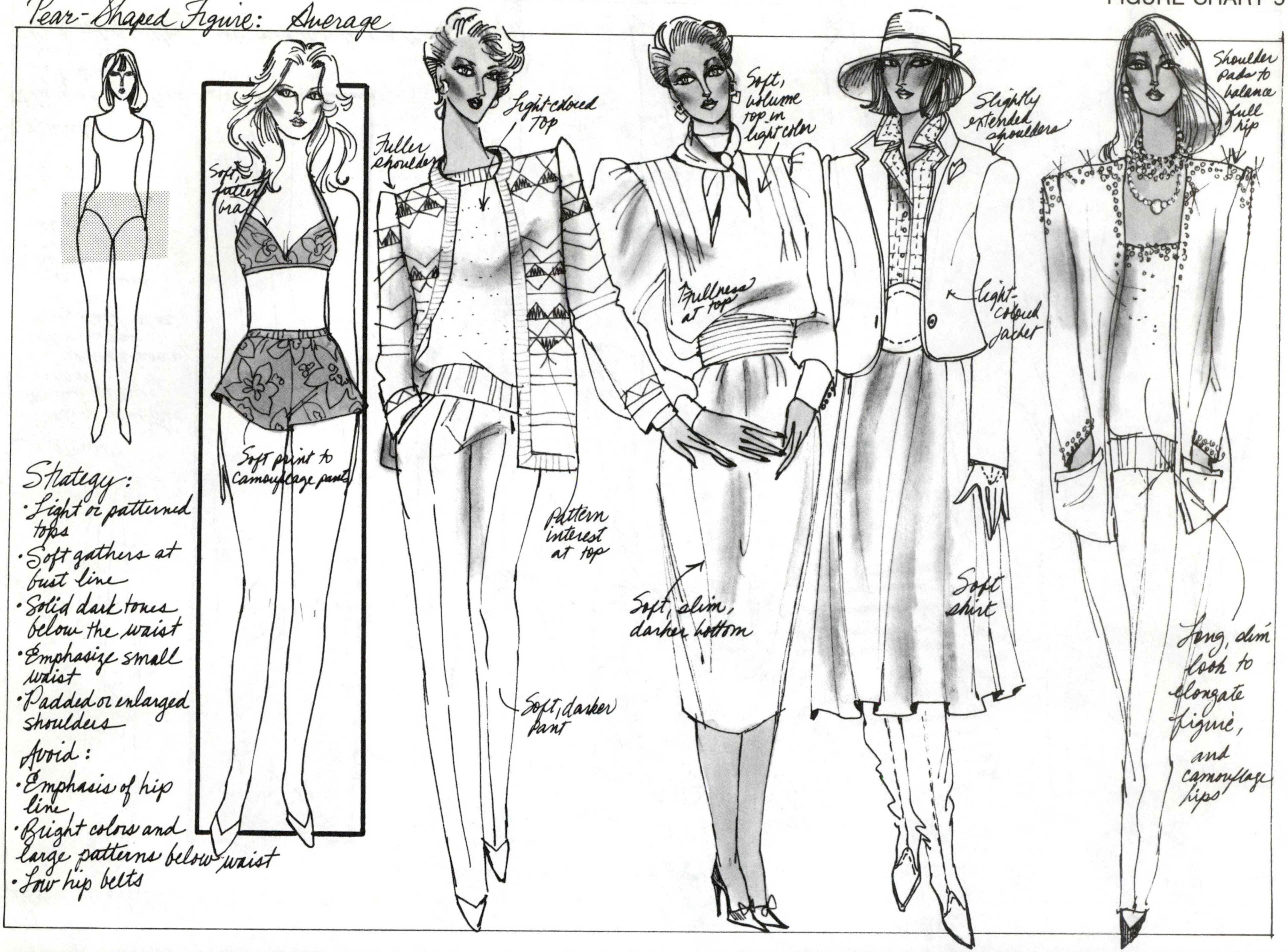

Pear-Shaped Figure: Average

Strategy:
- Light to patterned tops
- Soft gathers at bust line
- Solid dark tones below the waist
- Emphasize small waist
- Padded or enlarged shoulders

Avoid:
- Emphasis of hip line
- Bright colors and large patterns below waist
- Low hip belts

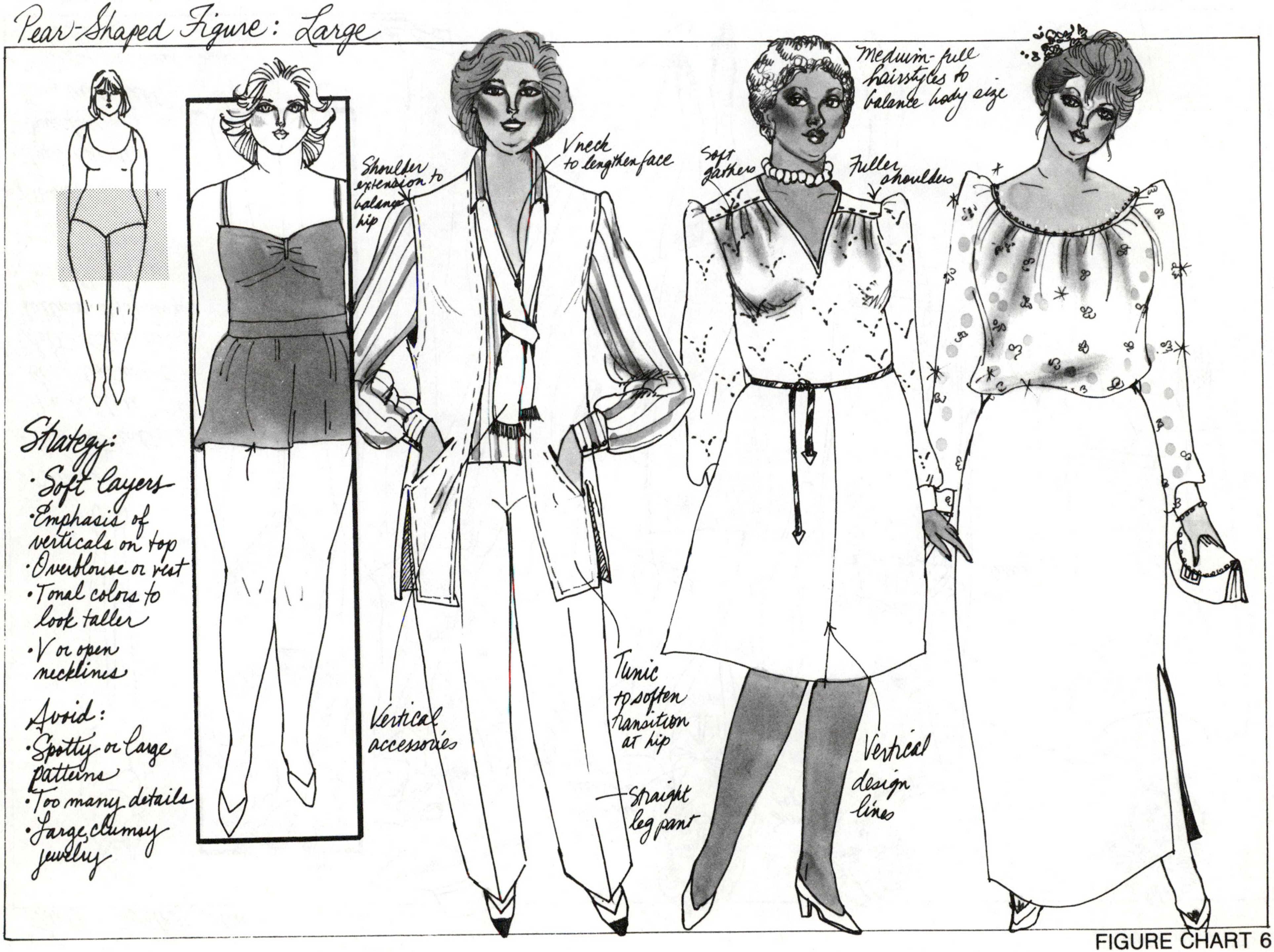
Pear-Shaped Figure: Large
Strategy:
·Soft layers
·Emphasis of verticals on top
·Overblouse or vest
·Tonal colors to look taller
·V or open necklines
Avoid:
·Spotty or large patterns
·Too many details
·Large, clumsy jewelry
Shoulder extension to balance hip
V neck to lengthen face
Vertical accessories
Tunic to soften transition at hip
Straight leg pant
Soft gathers
Fuller shoulders
Medium-full hairstyles to balance body size
Vertical design lines

FIGURE CHART 6

Full-Busted Figure: Thin

Hip curve and detail

Hip detail

Simple top

Soft fuller skirt

Demure neckline

No breast pockets

Hip details

Soft pleat pant

Strategy:
- Hip interest
- Hip belts to lengthen waist
- Soft gathers or fullness at hip line
- Low belts or hip design interest

Avoid:
- Full handos
- Smocks
- Very wide belts
- Brightly patterned tops

Full Busted Figure: Average

Smooth shoulder line

Jewelry for a long neck

Simple soft scarves

Fullness at lower arm

Soft Blouson

Hip detail

Soft, full skirt

Soft, full bodice without darts

Strategy:
- Soft skirts
- Pleated pants
- Soft blouses with lace
- Minimize waist-line definition
- Separate for best

Avoid:
- Front button plackets
- Plunging necklines • Full bodices • Wide belts
- Flowers on tops • Puffy sleeves

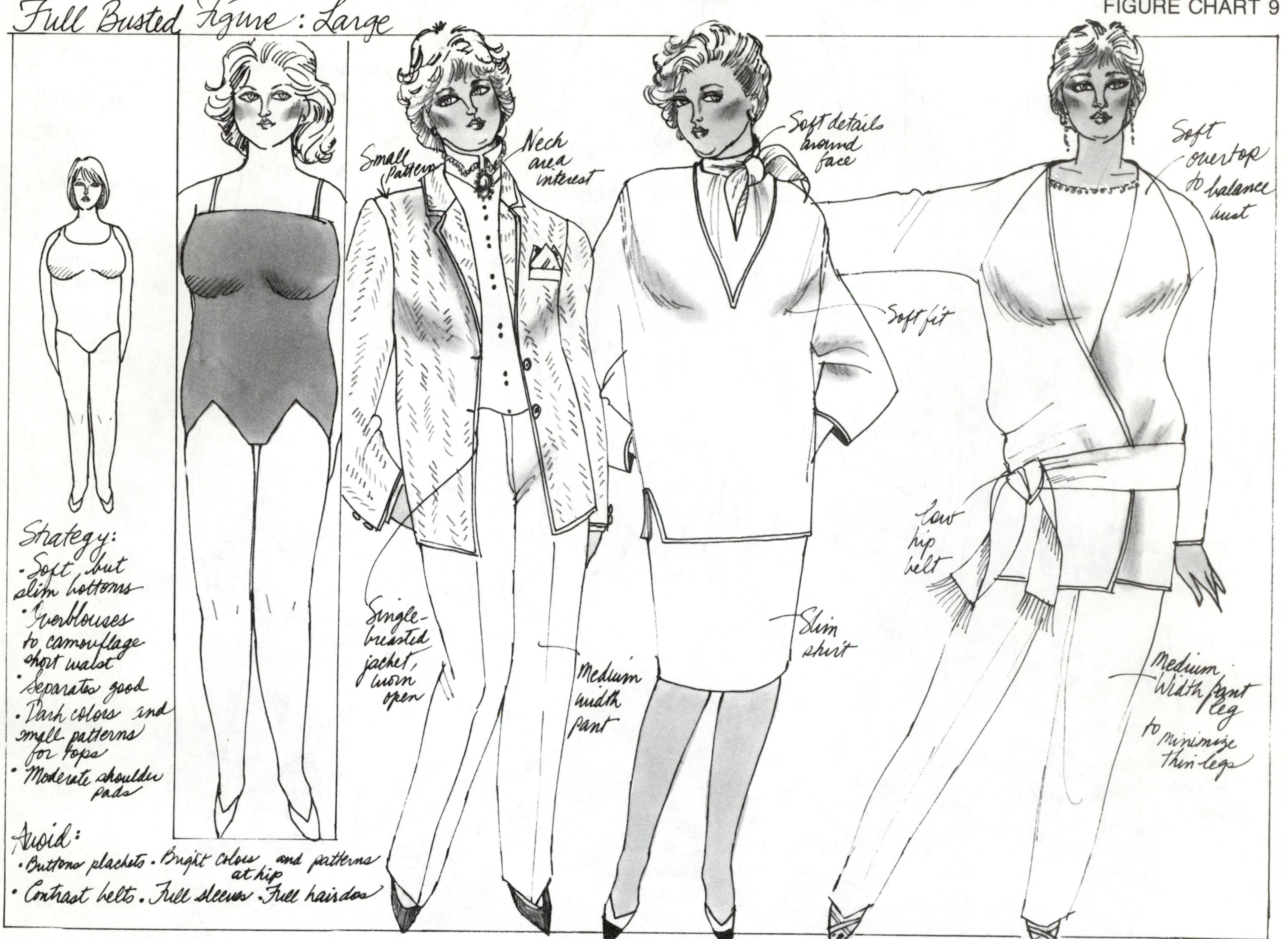

Full Busted Figure : Large

Soft overtop to balance bust

Medium width pant to minimize thin legs

Soft detail around face

Low hip belt

Soft fit

Slim skirt

Neck area interest

Medium width pant

Small pattern

Single-breasted jacket, worn open

Strategy:
- Soft but slim bottoms
- Overblouses to camouflage short waist
- Separates good
- Dark colors and small patterns for tops
- Moderate shoulder pads

Avoid:
- Button plackets · Bright colors and patterns at hip
- Contrast belts · Full sleeves, Full hairdos

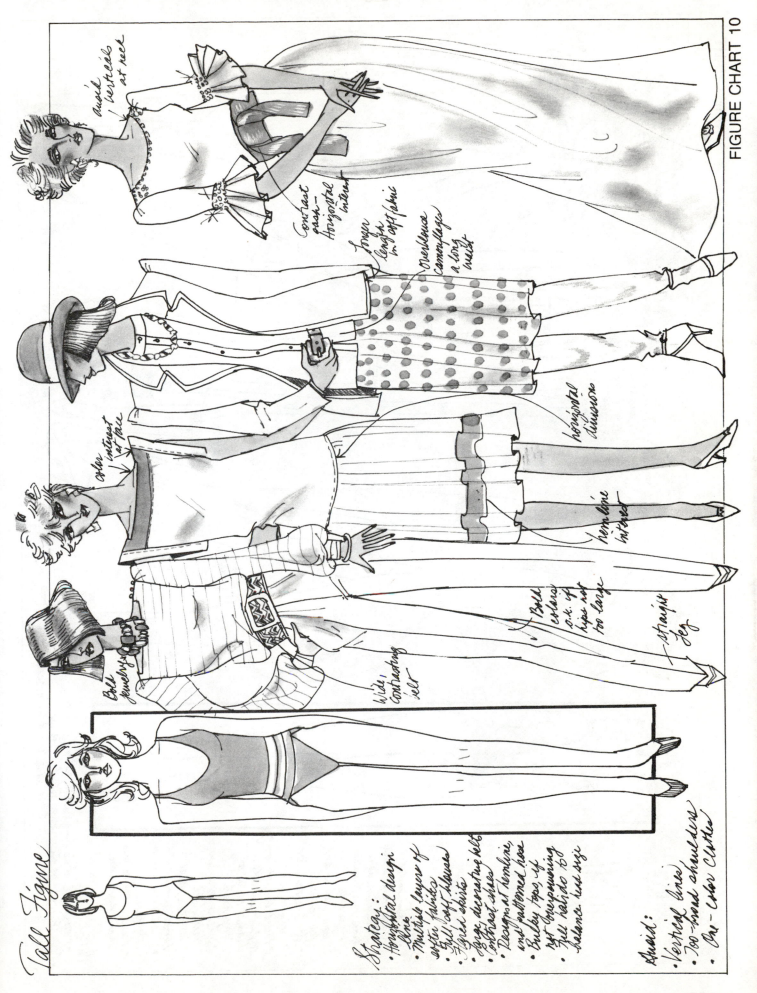

Tall Figure

avoid vertical at neck

Contrast area — horizontal interest

Long length in soft fabric

Overblouse camouflages a long waist

horizontal division

hemline interest

Color interest at face

Wide, contrasting belt

Bold jewelry, etc.

Bold colors o.k. if hips not too large

Straight leg

Strategy:
- Horizontal design lines
- Textured layers of different fabrics
- Full soft blouses
- Tiered skirts
- Large decorating with important shoes
- Designed hemline, and patterned hose
- Bulky tops if not overpowering
- Full bateau too
- balance head size

Avoid:
- Vertical lines
- Too-narrow shoulders
- One-color Clothes

Petite Figure

Delicate vertical design and simple line

Simple slim hairstyles and neat heels

Draw attention up towards the face

Strong simple verticals

Toned hose to match dress

No contrast to shoe

small patterns

Strategy:
- Stress vertical lines in garment
- Stress uneven lines and divisions in garment
- Tonal colors and few contrasts
- Scale details to a smaller figure
- Avoid overwhelming styles — use color dramatically to compensate
- Wear a medium to tall heel
- Smaller, neater hairstyles and hats
- Focus upward on the face
- Avoid contrasting shoe and hose

Avoid:
- Horizontal style lines • Contrasting colors
- Oversize garments • Large details • Large contrasting accessories

Short Waisted

Strategy:
- Narrow, trim belts, worn at the top of the hips
- Hip interest
- Ease the waist with a tunic or shirt
- Emphasize verticals
- Use a belt and a draped blouse that folds over belt

Avoid:
- Snugly fitted bodice
- Wide waist bands
- Contrasting belts
- Fitted suits

Loose areas in an overblouse

Moderate width

Wide, Contrasting belts

Long Waisted

Strategy:
- Wear large belts
- Ease the waist with a tunic
- Wear darker glows on top
- Emphasize horizontals
- Balance top with a dark color if torso is longer than legs

Avoid:
- Tops that are too short
- Insignificant waist detail — accent or leave it — do not be neutral

FIGURE CHART 12

189

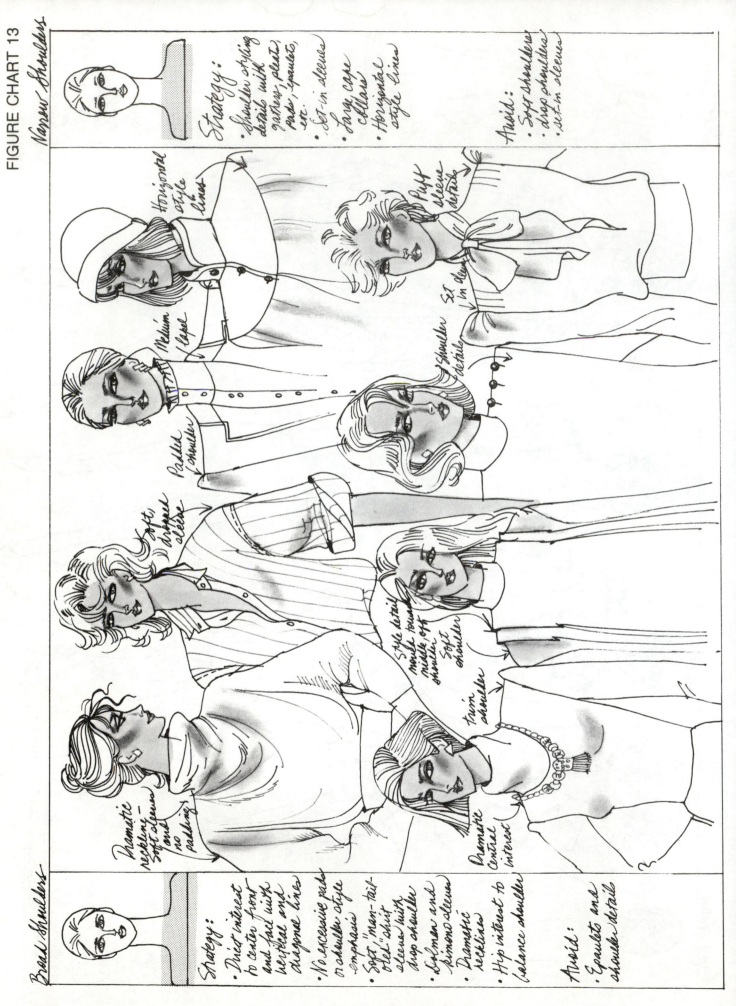

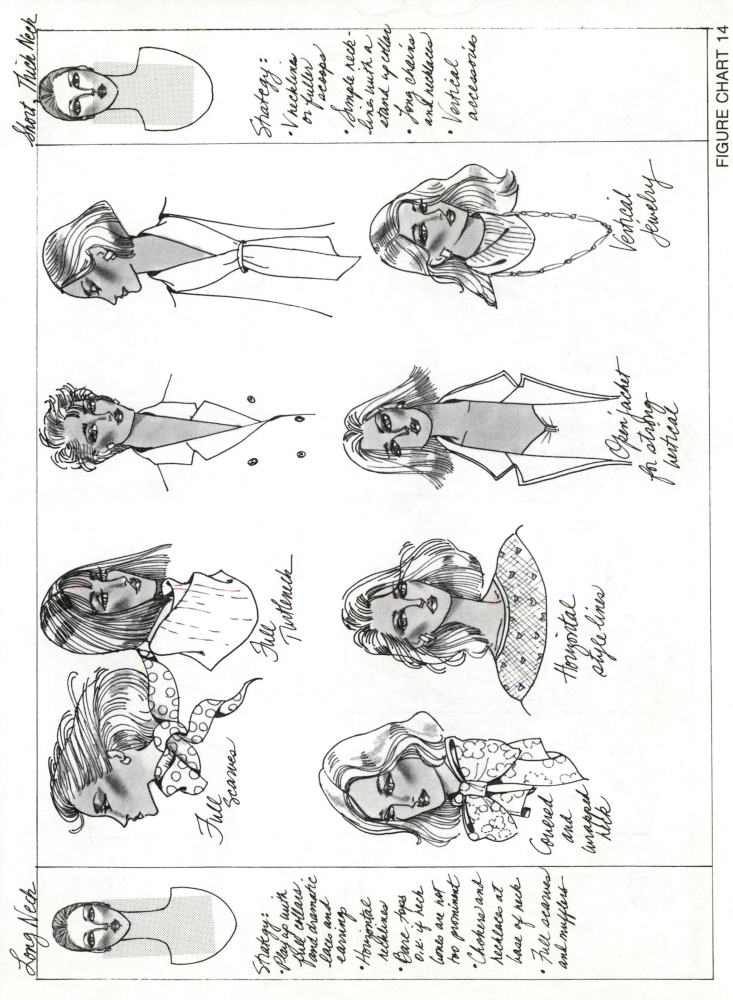

Short, Thick Neck

Strategy:
- V-neckline or fuller drapes
- Simple neck-line with a stand up collar
- Long chains and necklaces
- Vertical accessories

Vertical Jewelry

Open jacket for a long vertical

Full Turtleneck

Horizontal style lines

Full Scarves

Covered and wrapped with

Long Neck

Strategy:
- Play up with full collars band dramatic bows and earrings
- Horizontal necklines
- Bare tops o.k. if neck lines are not too prominent
- Chokers and necklace at base of neck
- Full scarves and mufflers

Pregnant Figure

Soft shaped styles

Tent shapes

Vertical accessories

Vertical style lines

Shoulder detail to balance tummy

Shirt long enough to extend height

Slim Pant Leg

Strategy:
• Focal interest on face and shoulders
• Emphasize verticals
• Use the fluid shape
• Comfortable shoes and lighter weight fabrics

Avoid:
• Tops that are too short
• Very snug garments
• Patterns or decor on the stomach